WINDOWS

WINDOWS

A COMEDY IN THREE ACTS
FOR IDEALISTS AND OTHERS

BY

JOHN GALSWORTHY

Fredonia Books
Amsterdam, The Netherlands

Windows
A Comedy in three acts
For idealist and others

by
John Galsworthy

ISBN 1-58963-029-7

Reprinted from the 1922 edition

Fredonia Books
Amsterdam, The Netherlands
http://www.FredoniaBooks.com

PERSONS OF THE PLAY

GEOFFREY MARCH	.	.	.	Freelance in Literature
JOAN MARCH	.	.	.	His Wife
MARY MARCH	.	.	.	Their Daughter
JOHNNY MARCH	.	.	.	Their Son
COOK	.	.	.	Their Cook
MR BLY	.	.	.	Their Window Cleaner
FAITH BLY	.	.	.	His Daughter
BLUNTER	.	.	.	A Strange Young Man
MR BARNABAS	.	.	.	In Plain Clothes

The action passes in Geoffrey March's House, Highgate—Spring-time.

ACT I. Thursday morning. The dining-room—after break-fast.

ACT II. Thurdsay, a fortnight later. The dining-room—after lunch.

ACT III. The same day. The dining-room—after dinner.

CAST OF THE ORIGINAL PRODUCTION

By Leon M. Lion and J. T. Grein,
At the Royal Court Theatre,
London, *April* 25, 1922

Geoffrey March	Herbert Marshall
Joan March	Irene Rooke
Mary March	Janet Eccles
Johnny March	John Howell
Cook	Clare Greet
Mr Bly	Ernest Thesiger
Faith	Mary Odette
Blunter	Leslie Banks
Mr Barnabas	C. R. Norris

ACT I

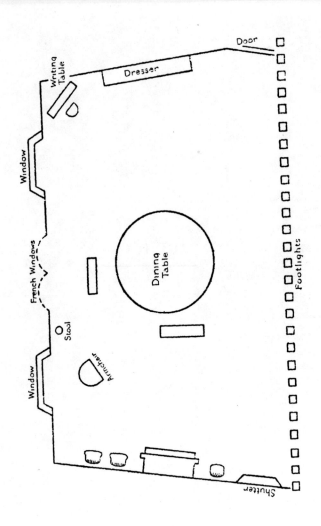

ACT I

The MARCH'S *dining-room opens through French windows on one of those gardens which seem infinite, till they are seen to be coterminous with the side walls of the house, and finite at the far end, because only the thick screen of acacias and sumachs prevents another house from being seen. The French and other windows form practically all the outer wall of that dining-room, and between them and the screen of trees lies the difference between the characters of Mr and Mrs March, with dots and dashes of Mary and Johnny thrown in. For instance, it has been formalised by* MRS MARCH *but the grass has not been cut by* MR MARCH, *and daffodils have sprung up there, which* MRS MARCH *desires for the dining-room, but of which* MR MARCH *says: " For God's sake, Joan, let them grow." About half therefore are now in a bowl on the breakfast table, and the other half still in the grass, in the compromise essential to lasting domesticity. A hammock under the acacias shows that* MARY *lies there sometimes with her eyes on the gleam of sunlight that comes through: and a trail in the longish grass, bordered with cigarette*

9

ends, proves that JOHNNY *tramps there with his
eyes on the ground or the stars, according. But
all this is by the way, because except for a yard
or two of gravel terrace outside the windows, it is
all painted on the backcloth. The* MARCHES *have
been at breakfast, and the round table, covered with
blue linen, is thick with remains, seven baskets full.
The room is gifted with old oak furniture : there
is a door, stage Left, Forward ; a hearth, where
a fire is burning, and a high fender on which one
can sit, stage Right, Middle ; and in the wall
below the fireplace, a service hatch covered with a
sliding shutter, for the passage of dishes into the
adjoining pantry. Against the wall, stage Left,
is an old oak dresser, and a small writing table
across the Left Back corner.* MRS MARCH *still
sits behind the coffee pot, making up her daily
list on tablets with a little gold pencil fastened to
her wrist. She is personable, forty-eight, trim,
well-dressed, and more matter-of-fact than seems
plausible.* MR MARCH *is sitting in an armchair,
sideways to the windows, smoking his pipe and
reading his newspaper, with little explosions to
which no one pays any attention, because it is
his daily habit. He is a fine-looking man of fifty
odd, with red-grey moustaches and hair, both of
which stiver partly by nature and partly because
his hands often push them up.* MARY *and*
JOHNNY *are close to the fireplace, stage Right.*
JOHNNY *sits on the fender, smoking a cigarette
and warming his back. He is a commonplace-*

looking young man, with a decided jaw, tall, neat, soulful, who has been in the war and writes poetry. MARY is less ordinary; you cannot tell exactly what is the matter with her. She too is tall, a little absent, fair, and well-looking. She has a small china dog in her hand, taken from the mantelpiece, and faces the audience. As the curtain rises she is saying in her soft and pleasant voice: " Well, what is the matter with us all, Johnny ? "

JOHNNY. Stuck, as we were in the trenches— like china dogs. [*He points to the ornament in her hand.*]

MR MARCH. [*Into his newspaper*] *Damn* these people !

MARY. If there isn't an ideal left, Johnny, it's no good pretending one.

JOHNNY. That's what I'm saying : Bankrupt !

MARY. What do you want ?

MRS MARCH. [*To herself*] Mutton cutlets. Johnny, will you be in to lunch ? [JOHNNY *shakes his head*] Mary ? [MARY *nods*] Geof ?

MR MARCH. [*Into his paper*] Swine !

MRS MARCH. That'll be three. [*To herself*] Spinach.

JOHNNY. If you'd just missed being killed for three blooming years for no spiritual result whatever, you'd want something to bite on, Mary.

MRS MARCH. [*Jotting*] Soap.

JOHNNY. What price the little and weak,

now ? Freedom and self-determination, and all that ?

MARY. Forty to one—no takers.

JOHNNY. It doesn't seem to worry *you*.

MARY. Well, what's the good ?

JOHNNY. Oh, you're a looker on, Mary.

MR MARCH. [*To his newspaper*] Of all God-forsaken time-servers !

> MARY *is moved so far as to turn and look over his shoulder a minute.*

JOHNNY. Who ?

MARY. Only the Old-Un.

MR MARCH. This is absolutely Prussian !

MRS MARCH. Soup, lobster, chicken salad. Go to Mrs Hunt's.

MR MARCH. And this fellow hasn't the nous to see that if ever there were a moment when it would pay us to take risks, and be generous—My hat ! He ought to be—knighted ! [*Resumes his paper.*]

JOHNNY. [*Muttering*] You see, even Dad can't suggest chivalry without talking of payment for it. That shows how we've sunk.

MARY. [*Contemptuously*] Chivalry ! Pouf ! Chivalry was " off " even before the war, Johnny. Who wants chivalry ?

JOHNNY. Of all shallow-pated humbug—that sneering at chivalry's the worst. Civilisation—such as we've got—is built on it.

MARY. [*Airily*] Then it's built on sand. [*She sits beside him on the fender.*]

JOHNNY. Sneering and smartness ! Pah !

MARY. [*Roused*] I'll tell you what, Johnny, it's mucking about with chivalry that makes your poetry rotten. [JOHNNY *seizes her arm and twists it*] Shut up—that hurts. [JOHNNY *twists it more*] You brute! [JOHNNY *lets her arm go.*]

JOHNNY. Ha! So you don't mind taking advantage of the fact that you can cheek me with impunity, because you're weaker. You've given the whole show away, Mary. Abolish chivalry and I'll make you sit up.

MRS MARCH. What are you two quarrelling about? Will you bring home cigarettes, Johnny—not Bogdogunov's Mamelukes—something more Anglo-American.

JOHNNY. All right! D'you want any more illustrations, Mary?

MARY. Pig! [*She has risen and stands rubbing her arm and recovering her placidity, which is considerable.*]

MRS MARCH. Geof, can you eat preserved peaches?

MR MARCH. Hell! What a policy! Um?

MRS MARCH. Can you eat preserved peaches?

MR MARCH. Yes. [*To his paper*] Making the country stink in the eyes of the world!

MARY. Nostrils, Dad, nostrils.

            MR MARCH *wriggles, half hearing.*

JOHNNY. [*Muttering*] Shallow idiots! Thinking we can do without chivalry!

MRS MARCH. I'm doing my best to get a parlour-maid, to-day, Mary, but these breakfast things won't clear themselves.

MARY. I'll clear them, Mother.

MRS MARCH. Good! [*She gets up. At the door*]
Knitting silk.   *She goes out.*

JOHNNY. Mother hasn't an ounce of idealism.
You might make her see stars, but never in the
singular.

MR MARCH. [*To his paper*] If God doesn't open
the earth soon——

MARY. Is there anything special, Dad ?

MR MARCH. This sulphurous government. [*He
drops the paper*] Give me a match, Mary.

        *As soon as the paper is out of his hands he
          becomes a different—an affable man.*

MARY. [*Giving him a match*] D'you mind writing
in here this morning, Dad ? Your study hasn't
been done. There's nobody but Cook.

MR MARCH. [*Lighting his pipe*] Anywhere.

        He slews the armchair towards the fire.

MARY. I'll get your things, then.

                      She goes out.

JOHNNY. [*Still on the fender*] What do you say,
Dad ? Is civilisation built on chivalry or on self-
interest ?

MR MARCH. The question is considerable, Johnny.
I should say it was built on contract, and jerry-built
at that.

JOHNNY. Yes; but why do we keep contracts
when we can break them with advantage and
impunity ?

MR MARCH. But do we keep them ?

JOHNNY. Well—say we do; otherwise you'll
admit there isn't such a thing as civilisation at

all. But *why* do we keep them ? For instance,
why don't we make Mary and Mother work for us
like Kafir women ? We could lick them into it.
Why did we give women the vote ? Why free
slaves ; why anything decent for the little and
weak ?

MR MARCH. Well, you might say it was convenient
for people living in communities.

JOHNNY. I don't think it's convenient at all.
I should like to make Mary sweat. Why not jungle
law, if there's nothing in chivalry.

MR MARCH. Chivalry is altruism, Johnny. Of
course it's quite a question whether altruism isn't
enlightened self-interest !

JOHNNY. Oh ! Damn !

> *The lank and shirt-sleeved figure of* MR BLY,
> *with a pail of water and cloths, has entered,*
> *and stands near the window, Left.*

BLY. Beg pardon, Mr March ; d'you mind me
cleanin' the winders here ?

MR MARCH. Not a bit.

JOHNNY. Bankrupt of ideals. That's it !

> MR BLY *stares at him, and puts his pail down*
> *by the window.*

> MARY *has entered with her father's writing*
> *materials which she puts on a stool beside*
> *him.*

MARY. Here you are, Dad ! I've filled up the ink
pot. Do be careful ! Come on, Johnny !

> *She looks curiously at* MR BLY, *who has*
> *begun operations at the bottom of the left-*

hand window, and goes, followed by
JOHNNY.

MR MARCH. [*Relighting his pipe and preparing his materials*] What do *you* think of things, Mr Bly ?

BLY. Not much, sir.

MR MARCH. Ah ! [*He looks up at* MR BLY, *struck by his large philosophical eyes and moth-eaten moustache*] Nor I.

BLY. I rather thought that, sir, from your writin's.

MR MARCH. Oh ! Do you read ?

BLY. I was at sea, once—formed the 'abit.

MR MARCH. Read any of my novels ?

BLY. Not to say all through—I've read some of your articles in the Sunday papers, though. Make you think !

MR MARCH. *I'm* at sea now—don't see dry land anywhere, Mr Bly.

BLY. [*With a smile*] That's right.

MR MARCH. D'you find that the general impression ?

BLY. No. People *don't* think. You 'ave to 'ave some cause for thought.

MR MARCH. Cause enough in the papers.

BLY. It's nearer 'ome with me. I've often thought I'd like a talk with you, sir. But I'm keepin' you. [*He prepares to swab the pane.*]

MR MARCH. Not at all. I enjoy it. Anything to put off work.

BLY. [*Looking at* MR MARCH, *then giving a wipe at the window*] What's drink to one is drought to another. I've seen two men take a drink out of the same can—one die of it and the other get off with a pain in his stomach.

MR MARCH. You've seen a lot, I expect.

BLY. Ah! I've been on the beach in my day. [*He sponges at the window*] It's given me a way o' lookin' at things that I don't find in other people. Look at the 'Ome Office. *They* got no philosophy.

MR MARCH. [*Pricking his ears*] What? Have you had dealings with them?

BLY. Over the reprieve that was got up for my daughter. But I'm keepin' you.

> *He swabs at the window, but always at the same pane, so that he does not advance at all.*

MR MARCH. Reprieve?

BLY. Ah! She was famous at eighteen. The *Sunday Mercury* was full of her, when she was in prison.

MR MARCH. [*Delicately*] Dear me! I'd no idea.

BLY. She's out now; been out a fortnight. I always say that fame's ephemereal. But she'll never settle to that weavin'. Her head got turned a bit.

MR MARCH. I'm afraid I'm in the dark, Mr Bly.

BLY. [*Pausing—dipping his sponge in the pail and then standing with it in his hand*] Why! Don't you remember the Bly case? They sentenced 'er to be 'anged by the neck until she was dead, for smotherin' her baby. She was only eighteen at the time of speakin'.

MR MARCH. Oh! yes! An inhuman business!

B

BLY. Ah! The jury recommended 'er to mercy. So they reduced it to Life.

MR MARCH. Life! Sweet Heaven!

BLY. That's what I said; so they give her two years. I don't hold with the *Sunday Mercury*, but it put *that* over. It's a misfortune to a girl to be good-lookin'.

MR MARCH. [*Rumpling his hair*] No, no! Dash it all! Beauty's the only thing left worth living for.

BLY. Well, I like to see green grass and a blue sky; but it's a mistake in a 'uman bein'. Look at any young chap that's good-lookin'—'e's doomed to the screen, or hair-dressin'. Same with the girls. My girl went into an 'airdresser's at seventeen and in six months she was in trouble. When I saw 'er with a rope round her neck, as you might say, I said to meself: "Bly," I said, "you're responsible for this— If she 'adn't been good-lookin'—it'd never 'ave 'appened."

> *During this speech* MARY *has come in with a tray, to clear the breakfast, and stands unnoticed at the dining-table, arrested by the curious words of* MR BLY.

MR MARCH. Your wife might not have thought that you were wholly the cause, Mr Bly.

BLY. Ah! My wife. She's passed on. But Faith—that's my girl's name—she never was like 'er mother; there's no 'eredity in 'er on that side.

MR MARCH. What sort of girl is she?

BLY. One for colour—likes a bit o' music—likes a dance. and a flower.

MARY. [*Interrupting softly*] Dad, I was going to clear, but I'll come back later.

MR MARCH. Come here and listen to this ! Here's a story to get your blood up ! How old was the baby, Mr Bly ?

BLY. Two days—'ardly worth mentionin'. They say she 'ad the 'ighstrikes after—an' when she comes to she says : " I've saved my baby's life." An' that's true enough when you come to think what that sort o' baby goes through as a rule ; dragged up by somebody else's hand, or took away by the Law. What can a workin' girl do with a baby born under the rose, as they call it ? Wonderful the difference money makes when it comes to bein' outside the Law.

MR MARCH. Right you are, Mr Bly. God's on the side of the big battalions.

BLY. Ah ! Religion ! [*His eyes roll philosophically*] Did you ever read 'Aigel ?

MR MARCH. Hegel, or Haeckel ?

BLY. Yes ; with an aitch. There's a balance abart 'im that I like. There's no doubt the Christian religion went too far. Turn the other cheek ! What oh ! An' this Anti-Christ, Neesha, what came in with the war—he went too far in the other direction. Neither of 'em practical men. You've got to strike a balance, and foller it.

MR MARCH. Balance ! Not much balance about us. We just run about and jump Jim Crow.

BLY. [*With a perfunctory wipe*] That's right ; we 'aven't got a faith these days. But what's the use of tellin' the Englishman to act like an angel.

He ain't either an angel or a blond beast. He's between the two, an 'ermumphradite. Take my daughter—— If I was a blond beast, I'd turn 'er out to starve ; if I was an angel, I'd starve meself to learn her the piano. I don't do either. Why ? Becos my instincts tells me not.

MR MARCH. Yes, but my doubt is whether our instincts at this moment of the world's history are leading us up or down.

BLY. What is up and what is down ? Can you answer me that ? Is it up or down to get so soft that you can't take care of yourself ?

MR MARCH. Down.

BLY. Well, is it up or down to get so 'ard that you can't take care of others ?

MR MARCH. Down.

BLY. Well, there you are !

MR MARCH. Then our instincts are taking us down ?

BLY. Nao. They're strikin' a balance, unbeknownst, all the time.

MR MARCH. You're a philosopher, Mr Bly.

BLY. [*Modestly*] Well, I do a bit in that line, too. In my opinion Nature made the individual believe he's goin' to live after 'e's dead just to keep 'im livin' while 'e's alive—otherwise he'd 'a died out.

MR MARCH. Quite a thought—quite a thought !

BLY. But I go one better than Nature. Follow your instincts is my motto.

MR MARCH. Excuse me, Mr Bly, I think Nature got hold of that before you.

BLY. [*Slightly chilled*] Well, I'm keepin' you.

MR MARCH. Not at all. You're a believer in conscience, or the little voice within. When my son was very small, his mother asked him once if he didn't hear a little voice within, telling him what was right. [MR MARCH *touches his diaphragm*] And he said: "I often hear little voices in here, but they never *say* anything." [MR BLY *cannot laugh, but he smiles*] Mary, Johnny must have been awfully like the Government.

BLY. As a matter of fact, I've got my daughter here—in obeyance.

MR MARCH. Where? I didn't catch.

BLY. In the kitchen. Your Cook told me you couldn't get hold of an 'ouse parlour-maid. So I thought it was just a chance—you bein' broadminded.

MR MARCH. Oh! I see. What would your mother say, Mary?

MARY. Mother would say: "Has she had experience?"

BLY. I've told you about her experience.

MR MARCH. Yes, but—as a parlour-maid.

BLY. Well! She can do hair. [*Observing the smile exchanged between* MR MARCH *and* MARY] And she's quite handy with a plate.

MR MARCH. [*Tentatively*] I'm a little afraid my wife would feel——

BLY. You see, in this weavin' shop—all the girls 'ave 'ad to be in trouble, otherwise they wouldn't take 'em. [*Apologetically towards* MARY] It's a kind of a disorderly 'ouse without the disorders. Excusin' the young lady's presence.

MARY. Oh! You needn't mind me, Mr Bly.

MR MARCH. And so you want her to come here? H'm!

BLY. Well I remember when she was a little bit of a thing—no higher than my knee—— [*He holds out his hand.*]

MR MARCH. [*Suddenly moved*] My God! yes. They've all been that. [*To* MARY] Where's your mother?

MARY. Gone to Mrs Hunt's. Suppose she's engaged one, Dad?

MR MARCH. Well, it's only a month's wages.

MARY. [*Softly*] She won't like it.

MR MARCH. Well, let's see her, Mr Bly; let's see her, if you don't mind.

BLY. Oh, I don't mind, sir, and she won't neither; she's used to bein' inspected by now. Why! she 'ad her bumps gone over just before she came out!

MR MARCH. [*Touched on the raw again*] H'm! Too bad! Mary, go and fetch her.

        MARY, *with a doubting smile, goes out.*

[*Rising*] You might give me the details of that trial, Mr Bly. I'll see if I can't write something that'll make people sit up. *That's* the way to send Youth to hell! How can a child who's had a rope round her neck—— !

BLY. [*Who has been fumbling in his pocket, produces some yellow paper-cuttings clipped together*] Here's

her references—the whole literature of the case.
And here's a letter from the chaplain in one of the
prisons sayin' she took a lot of interest in him ; a
nice young man, I believe. [*He suddenly brushes
a tear out of his eye with the back of his hand*] I never
thought I could 'a felt like I did over her bein' in
prison. Seemed a crool senseless thing—that pretty
girl o' mine. All over a baby that 'hadn't got used
to bein' alive. Tain't as if she'd been follerin' her
instincts ; why, she missed that baby something
crool.

MR MARCH. Of course, human life—even an
infant's——

BLY. I know you've got to 'ave a close time for
it. But when you come to think how they take
'uman life in Injia and Ireland, and all those other
places, it seems 'ard to come down like a cartload
o' bricks on a bit of a girl that's been carried away by
a moment's abiration.

MR MARCH. [*Who is reading the cuttings*] H'm !
What hypocrites we are !

BLY. Ah ! And 'oo can tell 'oo's the father ?
She never give us his name. I think the better of
'er for that.

MR MARCH. Shake hands, Mr Bly. So do I.
[BLY *wipes his hand, and* MR MARCH *shakes it*]
Loyalty's loyalty—especially when we men benefit
by it.

BLY. That's right, sir.

> MARY *has returned with* FAITH BLY, *who
> stands demure and pretty on the far side*

*of the table, her face an embodiment of
the pathetic watchful prison faculty of
adapting itself to whatever may be best for
its owner at the moment. At this moment
it is obviously best for her to look at the
ground, and yet to take in the faces of* MR
MARCH *and* MARY *without their taking
her face in. A moment, for all, of considerable embarrassment.*

MR MARCH. [*Suddenly*] Well, here we are !

> *The remark attracts* FAITH ; *she raises her
> eyes to his softly with a little smile, and
> drops them again.*

So you want to be our parlour-maid ?

FAITH. Yes, please.

MR MARCH. Well, Faith can remove mountains ;
but—er—I don't know if she can clear tables.

BLY. I've been tellin' Mr March and the young
lady what you're capable of. Show 'em what you
can do with a plate.

> FAITH *takes the tray from the sideboard and
> begins to clear the table, mainly by the light
> of nature. After a glance,* MR MARCH
> *looks out of the window and drums his
> fingers on the uncleaned pane.* MR BLY
> *goes on with his cleaning.* MARY, *after
> watching from the hearth, goes up and touches
> her father's arm.*

MARY. [*Between him and* MR BLY *who is bending
over his bucket, softly*] You're not watching, Dad.

MR MARCH. It's too pointed.

MARY. We've got to satisfy mother.

MR MARCH. I can satisfy her better if I don't look.

MARY. You're right.

> FAITH *has paused a moment and is watching them. As* MARY *turns, she resumes her operations.* MARY *joins, and helps her finish clearing, while the two men converse.*

BLY. Fine weather, sir, for the time of year.

MR MARCH. It is. The trees are growing.

BLY. Ah! I wouldn't be surprised to see a change of Government before long. I've seen 'uge trees in Brazil without any roots—seen 'em come down with a crash.

MR MARCH. Good image, Mr Bly. Hope you're right!

BLY. Well, Governments! They're all the same —Butter when they're out of power, and blood when they're in. And Lord! 'ow they do abuse other Governments for doin' the things they do themselves. Excuse me, I'll want her dosseer back, sir, when you've done with it.

MR MARCH. Yes, yes. [*He turns, rubbing his hands at the cleared table*] Well, that seems all right! And you can do hair?

FAITH. Oh! Yes, I can do hair. [*Again that little soft look, and smile so carefully adjusted.*]

MR MARCH. That's important, don't you think, Mary? [MARY, *accustomed to candour, smiles dubiously.*] [*Brightly*] Ah! And cleaning plate? What about that?

FAITH. Of course, if I had the opportunity——

MARY. You haven't—so far ?

FAITH. Only tin things.

MR MARCH. [*Feeling a certain awkwardness*] Well, I daresay we can find some for you. Can you—er—be firm on the telephone ?

FAITH. Tell them you're engaged when you're not ? Oh ! yes.

MR MARCH. Excellent ! Let's see, Mary, what else is there ?

MARY. Waiting, and house work.

MR MARCH. Exactly.

FAITH. I'm very quick. I—I'd like to come. [*She looks down*] I don't care for what I'm doing now. It makes you feel your position.

MARY. Aren't they nice to you ?

FAITH. Oh ! yes—kind ; but— [*She looks up*] it's against my instincts.

MR MARCH. Oh ! [*Quizzically*] You've got a disciple, Mr Bly.

BLY. [*Rolling his eyes at his daughter*] Ah ! but you mustn't 'ave instincts here, you know. You've got a chance, and you must come to stay, and do yourself credit.

FAITH. [*Adapting her face*] Yes, I know, I'm very lucky.

MR MARCH. [*Deprecating thanks and moral precept*] That's all right ! Only, Mr Bly, I can't absolutely answer for Mrs March. She may think——

MARY. There *is* Mother ; I heard the door.

BLY. [*Taking up his pail*] I quite understand,

sir ; I've been a married man myself. It's very queer
the way women look at things. I'll take her away
now, and come back presently and do these other
winders. You can talk it over by yourselves. But
if you do see your way, sir, I shan't forget it in an
'urry. To 'ave the responsibility of her—really,
it's dreadful.

> FAITH'S *face has grown sullen during this*
> *speech, but it clears up in another little*
> *soft look at* MR MARCH, *as she and* MR BLY
> *go out.*

MR MARCH. Well, Mary, have I done it ?

MARY. You have, Dad.

MR MARCH. [*Running his hands through his hair*]
Pathetic little figure ! Such infernal inhumanity !

MARY. How are you going to put it to
mother ?

MR MARCH. Tell her the story, and pitch it
strong.

MARY. Mother's not impulsive.

MR MARCH. We *must* tell her, or she'll think me
mad.

MARY. She'll do that, anyway, dear.

MR MARCH. Here she is ! Stand by !

> *He runs his arm through* MARY'S, *and they*
> *sit on the fender, at bay.* MRS MARCH
> *enters, Left.*

MR MARCH. Well, what luck ?

MRS MARCH. None.

MR MARCH. [*Unguardedly*] Good !

MRS MARCH. What ?

MR MARCH. [*Cheerfully*] Well, the fact is, Mary and I have caught one for you; Mr Bly's daughter——

MRS MARCH. Are you out of your senses? Don't you know that she's the girl who——

MR MARCH. That's it. She wants a lift.

MRS MARCH. Geof!

MR MARCH. Well, don't we want a maid?

MRS MARCH. [*Ineffably*] Ridiculous!

MR MARCH. We tested her, didn't we, Mary?

MRS MARCH. [*Crossing to the bell, and ringing*] You'll just send for Mr Bly and get rid of her again.

MR MARCH. Joan, if we comfortable people can't put ourselves a little out of the way to give a helping hand——

MRS MARCH. To girls who smother their babies?

MR MARCH. Joan, I revolt. I won't be a hypocrite and a Pharisee.

MRS MARCH. Well, for goodness sake let *me* be one.

MARY. [*As the door opens*]. Here's Cook!

     COOK *stands—sixty, stout, and comfortable—
         with a crumpled smile.*

COOK. Did you ring, ma'am?

MR MARCH. We're in a moral difficulty, Cook, so naturally we come to you.

                        COOK *beams.*

MRS MARCH. [*Impatiently*] Nothing of the sort, Cook; it's a question of common sense.

COOK. Yes, ma'am.

Mrs March. That girl, Faith Bly, wants to come here as parlour-maid. Absurd !

Mr March. You know her story, Cook ? I want to give the poor girl a chance. Mrs March thinks it's *taking* chances. What do you say ?

Cook. Of course, it is a risk, sir ; but there ! you've got to take 'em to get maids nowadays. If it isn't in the past, it's in the future. I daresay I could learn 'er.

Mrs March. It's not her work, Cook, it's her instincts. A girl who smothered a baby that she oughtn't to have had——

Mr March. [*Remonstrant*] If she hadn't had it how could she have smothered it ?

Cook. [*Soothingly*] Perhaps she's repented, ma'am.

Mrs March. Of course she's repented. But did you ever know repentance change anybody, Cook ?

Cook. [*Smiling*] Well, generally it's a way of gettin' ready for the next.

Mrs March. Exactly.

Mr March. If we never get another chance *because* we repent——

Cook. I always think of Master Johnny, ma'am, and my jam ; he used to repent so beautiful, dear little feller—such a conscience ! I never could bear to lock it away.

Mrs March. Cook, you're wandering. I'm surprised at your encouraging the idea ; I really am.

COOK *plaits her hands.*

MR MARCH. Cook's been in the family longer than I have—haven't you, Cook ? [COOK *beams*] She knows much more about a girl like that than we do.

COOK. We had a girl like her, I remember, in your dear mother's time, Mr Geoffrey.

MR MARCH. How did she turn out ?

COOK. Oh ! She didn't.

MRS MARCH. There !

MR MARCH. Well, I can't bear behaving like everybody else. Don't you think we might give her a chance, Cook ?

COOK. My 'eart says yes, ma'am.

MR MARCH. Ha !

COOK. And my 'ead says no, sir.

MRS MARCH. Yes !

MR MARCH. Strike your balance, Cook.

> COOK *involuntarily draws her joined hands sharply in upon her amplitude.*

Well ? . . . I didn't catch the little voice within.

COOK. Ask Master Johnny, sir ; he's been in the war.

MR MARCH. [*To* MARY] Get Johnny.

> MARY *goes out.*

MRS MARCH. What on earth has the war to do with it ?

COOK. The things he tells me, ma'am, is too wonderful for words. He's 'ad to do with prisoners and generals, every sort of 'orror.

MR MARCH. Cook's quite right. The war destroyed all our ideals and probably created the baby.

MRS MARCH. It didn't smother it ; or condemn the girl.

MR MARCH. [*Running his hands through his hair*] The more I think of that——! [*He turns away.*]

MRS MARCH. [*Indicating her husband*] You see, Cook, that's the mood in which I have to engage a parlour-maid. What am I to do with your master ?

COOK. It's an 'ealthy rage, ma'am.

MRS MARCH. I'm tired of being the only sober person in this house.

COOK. [*Reproachfully*] Oh ! ma'am, I never touch a drop.

MRS MARCH. I didn't mean anything of that sort. But they do break out so.

COOK. Not Master Johnny.

MRS MARCH. Johnny ! He's the worst of all. His poetry is nothing but one long explosion.

MR MARCH. [*Coming from the window*] I say : We ought to have faith and jump.

MRS MARCH. If we do have Faith, we shall jump.

COOK. [*Blankly*] Of course, in the Bible they 'ad faith, and just look what it did to them !

MR MARCH. I mean faith in human instincts, human nature, Cook.

COOK. [*Scandalised*] Oh ! no, sir, *not* human nature ; I never let that get the upper hand.

MR MARCH. You talk to Mr Bly. He's a remarkable man.

Cook. I do, sir, every fortnight when he does the kitchen windows.

Mr March. Well, doesn't he impress you ?

Cook. Ah ! When he's got a drop o' stout in 'im—Oh ! dear ! [*She smiles placidly.*]

JOHNNY *has come in.*

Mr March. Well, Johnny, has Mary told you ?

Mrs March. [*Looking at his face*] Now, my dear boy, don't be hasty and foolish !

Johnny. Of course you ought to take her, Mother.

Mrs March. [*Fixing him*] Have you seen her, Johnny ?

Johnny. She's in the hall, poor little devil, waiting for her sentence.

Mrs March. There are plenty of other chances, Johnny.   Why on earth should we—— ?

Johnny. Mother, it's just an instance. When something comes along that takes a bit of doing—Give it to the other chap !

Mr March. Bravo, Johnny !

Mrs March. [*Drily*] Let me see, which of us will have to put up with her shortcomings—Johnny or I ?

Mary. She looks quick, Mother.

Mrs March. Girls pick up all sorts of things in prison. We can hardly expect her to be honest. You don't mind that, I suppose ?

Johnny. It's a chance to make something decent out of her.

Mrs March. I can't understand this passion for vicarious heroism, Johnny.

JOHNNY. Vicarious !

MRS MARCH. Well, where do you come in ? You'll make poems about the injustice of the Law. Your father will use her in a novel. She'll wear Mary's blouses, and everybody will be happy—except Cook and me.

MR MARCH. Hang it all, Joan, you might be the Great Public itself !

MRS MARCH. I am—get all the kicks and none of the ha'pence.

JOHNNY. We'll all help you.

MRS MARCH. For Heaven's sake—no, Johnny !

MR MARCH. Well, make up your mind !

MRS MARCH. It was made up long ago.

JOHNNY. [*Gloomily*] The more I see of things the more disgusting they seem. I don't see what we're living for. All right. Chuck the girl out, and let's go rooting along with our noses in the dirt.

MR MARCH. Steady, Johnny !

JOHNNY. Well, Dad, there was one thing anyway we learned out there— When a chap was in a hole —to pull him out, even at a risk.

MRS MARCH. There are people who—the moment you pull them out—jump in again.

MARY. We can't tell till we've tried, Mother.

COOK. It's wonderful the difference good food'll make, ma'am.

MRS MARCH. Well, you're all against me. Have it your own way, and when you regret it—remember me !

MR MARCH. We will—we will ! That's settled,

C

then. Bring her in and tell her. We'll go on to
the terrace.

> *He goes out through the window, followed by*
> JOHNNY.

MARY. [*Opening the door*] Come in, please.

> FAITH *enters and stands beside* COOK, *close*
> *to the door.* MARY *goes out.*

MRS MARCH. [*Matter of fact in defeat as in victory*]
You want to come to us, I hear.

FAITH. Yes.

MRS MARCH. And you don't know much ?

FAITH. No.

COOK. [*Softly*] Say ma'am, dearie.

MRS MARCH. Cook is going to do her best for you.
Are you going to do yours for us ?

FAITH. [*With a quick look up*] Yes—ma'am.

MRS MARCH. Can you begin at once ?

FAITH. Yes.

MRS MARCH. Well, then, Cook will show you where
things are kept, and how to lay the table and that.
Your wages will be thirty until we see where we
are. Every other Sunday, and Thursday afternoon.
What about dresses ?

FAITH. [*Looking at her dress*] I've only got this—
I had it before, of course, it hasn't been worn.

MRS MARCH. Very neat. But I meant for the
house. You've no money, I suppose ?

FAITH. Only one pound thirteen, ma'am.

MRS MARCH. We shall have to find you some
dresses, then. Cook will take you to-morrow to
Needham's. You needn't wear a cap unless you

like. Well, I hope you'll get on. I'll leave you
with Cook now.

> *After one look at the girl, who is standing
> motionless, she goes out.*

FAITH. [*With a jerk, as if coming out of plaster of
Paris*] She's never been in prison!

COOK. [*Comfortably*] Well, my dear, we can't all
of us go everywhere, 'owever 'ard we try!

> *She is standing back to the dresser, and turns
> to it, opening the right-hand drawer.*

COOK. Now, 'ere's the wine. The master likes
'is glass. And 'ere's the spirits in the tantaliser—
'tisn't ever kept locked, in case Master Johnny
should bring a friend in. Have you noticed Master
Johnny? [FAITH *nods*] Ah! He's a dear boy; and
wonderful high-principled since he's been in the war.
He'll come to me sometimes and say: "Cook,
we're all going to the devil!" They think 'ighly
of 'im as a poet. He spoke up for you beautiful.

FAITH. Oh! He spoke up for me?

COOK. Well, of course they had to talk you
over.

FAITH. I wonder if they think I've got feelings.

COOK. [*Regarding her moody, pretty face*] Why!
We all have feelin's!

FAITH. Not below three hundred a year.

COOK. [*Scandalised*] Dear, dear! Where were you
educated?

FAITH. I wasn't.

COOK. Tt! Well—it's wonderful what a change
there is in girls since my young days [*Pulling out*

a drawer] Here's the napkins. You change the master's every day at least because of his moustache ; and the others every two days, but always clean ones Sundays.   Did you keep Sundays in *there* ?

FAITH. [*Smiling*] Yes. Longer chapel.

COOK. It'll be a nice change for you, here. They don't go to Church ; they're agnosticals. [*Patting her shoulder*] How old are you ?

FAITH. Twenty.

COOK. Think of that—and such a life ! Now, dearie, I'm your friend. Let the present bury the past—as the sayin' is. Forget all about yourself, and you'll be a different girl in no time.

FAITH. Do you want to be a different woman ?

> COOK *is taken flat aback by so sudden a revelation of the pharisaism of which she has not been conscious.*

COOK. Well ! You *are* sharp ! [*Opening another dresser drawer*] Here's the vinegar ! And here's the sweets, and [*rather anxiously*] you mustn't eat them.

FAITH. I wasn't in for theft.

COOK. [*Shocked at such rudimentary exposure of her natural misgivings*] No, no ! But girls have appetites.

FAITH. *They* didn't get much chance where I've been.

COOK. Ah ! You must tell me all about it. Did you have adventures ?

FAITH. There isn't such a thing in a prison.

COOK. You don't say ! Why, in the books they're

escapin' all the time. But books is books ; I've always said so. How were the men ?

FAITH. Never saw a man—only a chaplain.

COOK. Dear, dear ! They must be quite fresh to you, then ! How long was it ?

FAITH. Two years.

COOK. And never a day out ? What did you do all the time ? Did they learn you anything ?

FAITH. Weaving. That's why I hate it.

COOK. Tell me about your poor little baby. I'm sure you meant it for the best.

FAITH. [*Sardonically*] Yes ; I was afraid they'd make it a ward in Chancery.

COOK. Oh ! dear—what things do come into your head ! Why ! No one can take a baby from its mother.

FAITH. Except the Law.

COOK. Tt ! Tt ! Well ! Here's the pickled onions. Miss Mary loves 'em ! Now then, let me see you lay the cloth.

> *She takes a tablecloth out, hands it to* FAITH, *and while the girl begins to unfold the cloth she crosses to the service shutter.*

And here's where we pass the dishes through into the pantry.

> *The door is opened, and* MRS MARCH'S *voice says :* " Cook—a minute ! "

[*Preparing to go*] Salt cellars one at each corner— four, and the peppers. [*From the door*] Now the decanters. Oh ! you'll soon get on. [MRS MARCH : " Cook ! "] Yes, ma'am.

She goes.

FAITH, *left alone, stands motionless, biting her pretty lip, her eyes mutinous. Hearing footsteps, she looks up.* MR BLY, *with his pail and cloths, appears outside.*

BLY. [*Preparing to work, while* FAITH *prepares to set the salt cellars*] So you've got it ! You never know your luck. Up to-day and down to-morrow. I'll 'ave a glass over this to-night. What d'you get ?

FAITH. Thirty.

BLY. It's not the market price, still, you're not the market article. Now, put a good heart into it and get to know your job ; you'll find Cook full o' philosophy if you treat her right—she can make a dumplin' with anybody. But look 'ere ; you confine yourself to the ladies !

FAITH. I don't want your advice, father.

BLY. I know parents are out of date ; still, I've put up with a lot on your account, so gimme a bit of me own back.

FAITH. I don't know whether I shall like this. I've been shut up so long. I want to see some life.

BLY. Well, that's natural. But I want you to do well. I suppose you'll be comin' 'ome to fetch your things to-night ?

FAITH. Yes.

BLY. I'll have a flower for you. What'd you like—daffydils ?

FAITH. No ; one with a scent to it.

BLY. I'll ask at Mrs Bean's round the corner.

She'll pick 'em out from what's over. Never 'ad much nose for a flower meself. I often thought you'd like a flower when you was in prison.

FAITH. [*A little touched*] Did you? Did you—really?

BLY. Ah! I suppose I've drunk more glasses over your bein' in there than over anything that ever 'appened to me. Why! I · couldn't relish the war for it! And I suppose you 'ad none to relish. Well, it's over. So, put an 'eart into it.

FAITH. I'll try.

BLY. "There's compensation for everything"—'Aigel says. At least, if it wasn't 'Aigel it was one o' the others. I'll move on to the study now. Ah! He's got some winders there lookin' right over the country. And a wonderful lot o' books, if you feel inclined for a read one of these days.

COOK'S VOICE. Faith!

> FAITH *sets down the salt cellar in her hand, puts her tongue out a very little, and goes out into the hall.* MR BLY *is gathering up his pail and cloths when* MR MARCH *enters at the window.*

MR MARCH. So it's fixed up, Mr Bly.

BLY. [*Raising himself*] I'd like to shake your 'and, sir. [*They shake hands*] It's a great weight off my mind.

MR MARCH. It's rather a weight on my wife's, I'm afraid. But we must hope for the best. The country wants rain, but—I doubt if we shall get it with this Government.

BLY. Ah ! We want the good old times—when
you could depend on the seasons. The further you
look back the more dependable the times get ; 'ave
you noticed that, sir ?

MR MARCH. [*Suddenly*] Suppose they'd hanged
your daughter, Mr Bly. What would you have
done ?

BLY. Well, to be quite frank; I should 'ave got
drunk on it.

MR MARCH. Public opinion's always in advance
of the Law. I think your daughter's a most pathetic
little figure.

BLY. Her looks *are* against her. I never found a
man that didn't.

MR MARCH. [*A little disconcerted*] Well, we'll try
and give her a good show here.

BLY. [*Taking up his pail*] I'm greatly obliged ;
she'll appreciate anything you can do for her. [*He
moves to the door and pauses there to say*] Fact is—
her winders wants cleanin', she 'ad a dusty time in
there.

MR MARCH. I'm sure she had.

> MR BLY *passes out, and* MR MARCH *busies
> himself in gathering up his writing things
> preparatory to seeking his study. While
> he is so engaged* FAITH *comes in.
> Glancing at him, she resumes her placing
> of the decanters, as* JOHNNY *enters by the
> window, and comes down to his father by
> the hearth.*

JOHNNY. [*Privately*] If you haven't begun your

morning, Dad, you might just tell me what you
think of these verses.

> *He puts a sheet of notepaper before his father,
> who takes it and begins to con over the
> verses thereon, while* JOHNNY *looks care-
> fully at his nails.*

MR MARCH. Er—I—I like the last line awfully,
Johnny.

JOHNNY. [*Gloomily*] What about the other eleven ?

MR MARCH. [*Tentatively*] Well—old man, I—er
—think perhaps it'd be stronger if they were out.

JOHNNY. Good God !

> *He takes back the sheet of paper, clutches his
> brow, and crosses to the door. As he
> passes* FAITH, *she looks up at him with
> eyes full of expression.* JOHNNY *catches
> the look, jibs ever so little, and goes out.*

COOK'S VOICE. [*Through the door, which is still
ajar*] Faith !

> FAITH *puts the decanters on the table, and
> goes quickly out.*

MR MARCH. [*Who has seen this little by-play—to
himself—in a voice of dismay*] Oh ! oh ! I wonder !

CURTAIN.

ACT II

ACT II

A fortnight later in the MARCH'S dining-room; a day of violent April showers. Lunch is over and the table littered with remains—twelve baskets full.

MR MARCH *and* MARY *have lingered.* MR MARCH *is standing by the hearth where a fire is burning, filling a fountain pen.* MARY *sits at the table opposite, pecking at a walnut.*

MR MARCH. [*Examining his fingers*] What it is to have an inky present! Suffer with me, Mary!

MARY. " Weep ye no more, sad Fountains!
Why need ye flow so fast ? "

MR MARCH. [*Pocketing his pen*] Coming with me to the British Museum ? I want to have a look at the Assyrian reliefs.

MARY. Dad, have you noticed Johnny ?

MR MARCH. I have.

MARY. Then only Mother hasn't.

MR MARCH. I've always found your mother extremely good at seeming not to notice things, Mary.

MARY. Faith ! She's got on very fast this fortnight.

45

Mr March. The glad eye, Mary. I got it that first morning.

Mary. *You*, Dad?

Mr March. No, no! Johnny got it, and I got him getting it.

Mary. What are you going to do about it?

Mr March. What *does* one do with a glad eye that belongs to some one else?

Mary. [*Laughing*] No. But, seriously, Dad, Johnny's not like you and me. Why not speak to Mr Bly?

Mr March. Mr Bly's eyes are not glad.

Mary. Dad! Do be serious! Johnny's capable of anything except a sense of humour.

Mr March. The girl's past makes it impossible to say anything to her.

Mary. Well, I warn you. Johnny's very queer just now; he's in the "lose the world to save your soul" mood. It really is *too* bad of that girl. After all, we did what most people wouldn't.

Mr March. Come! Get your hat on, Mary, or we shan't make the Tube before the next shower.

Mary. [*Going to the door*] Something must be done.

Mr March. As you say, something—— Ah! Mr Bly!

> Mr Bly, *in precisely the same case as a fortnight ago, with his pail and cloths, is coming in.*

Bly. Afternoon, sir! Shall I be disturbing you if I do the winders here?

MR MARCH. Not at all.

           MR BLY *crosses to the windows.*

MARY. [*Pointing to* MR BLY'S *back*] Try !

BLY. Showery, sir.

MR MARCH. Ah !

BLY. Very tryin' for winders. [*Resting*] My daughter givin' satisfaction, I hope ?

MR MARCH. [*With difficulty*] Er—in her work, I believe, coming on well. But the question is, Mr Bly, do—er—any of us ever really give satisfaction except to ourselves ?

BLY. [*Taking it as an invitation to his philosophical vein*] Ah ! that's one as goes to the roots of 'uman nature. There's a lot of disposition in all of us. And what I always say is : One man's disposition is another man's indisposition.

MR MARCH. By George ! Just hits the mark.

BLY. [*Filling his sponge*] Question is : How far are you to give rein to your disposition ? When I was in Durban, Natal, I knew a man who had the biggest disposition I ever come across. 'E struck 'is wife, 'e smoked opium, 'e was a liar, 'e gave all the rein 'e could, and yet withal one of the pleasantest men I ever met.

MR MARCH. Perhaps in giving rein he didn't strike you.

BLY. [*With a big wipe, following his thought*] He said to me once : " Joe," he said, " if I was to hold meself in, I should be a devil." There's where you get it. Policemen, priests, prisoners. Cab'net Ministers, any one who leads an unnatural life, see

how it twists 'em. You can't suppress a thing
without it swellin' you up in another place.

Mr March. And the moral of that is—— ?

Bly. Follow your instincts. You see—if I'm not
keepin' you—now that we ain't got no faith, as we
were sayin' the other day, no Ten Commandments
in black an' white—we've just got to be 'uman bein's
—raisin' Cain, and havin' feelin' hearts. What's
the use of all these lofty ideas that you can't live
up to ? Liberty, Fraternity, Equality, Democracy
—see what comes o' fightin' for 'em ! 'Ere we
are—wipin' out the lot. We thought they was
fixed stars ; they was only comets—hot air. No ;
trust 'uman nature, I say, and follow your
instincts.

Mr March. We were talking of your daughter—
I—I——

Bly. There's a case in point. Her instincts was
starved goin' on for three years, because, mind you,
they kept her hangin' about in prison months before
they tried her. I read your article, and I thought
to meself after I'd finished : Which would I feel
smallest—if I was—the Judge, the Jury, or the
'Ome Secretary ? It *was* a treat, that article !
They ought to abolish that in'uman " To be hanged
by the neck until she is dead." It's my belief they
only keep it because it's poetry ; that and the wigs
—they're hard up for a bit of beauty in the Courts
of Law. Excuse my 'and, sir ; I do thank you
for that article.

He extends his wiped hand, which Mr March

*shakes with the feeling that he is always
shaking* Mr Bly's *hand.*

Mr March. But, *àpropos* of your daughter, Mr Bly.
I suppose none of us ever change our natures.

Bly. [*Again responding to the appeal that he senses
to his philosophical vein*] Ah ! but 'oo can see what
our natures are ? Why, I've known people that
could see nothin' but theirselves and their own
families, unless they was drunk. At my daughter's
trial, I see right into the lawyers, judge and all.
There she was, hub of the whole thing, and all they
could see of her was 'ow far she affected 'em personally
—one tryin' to get 'er guilty, the other tryin' to
get 'er off, and the judge summin' 'er up cold-
blooded.

Mr March. But that's what they're paid for,
Mr Bly.

Bly. Ah ! But which of 'em was thinkin' :
" 'Ere's a little bit o' warm life on its own. 'Ere's
a little dancin' creature. What's she feelin', wot's
'er complaint ? "—impersonal-like. I like to see
a man do a bit of speculatin', with his mind off of
'imself, for once.

Mr March. " The man that hath not speculation
in his soul."

Bly. That's right, sir. When I see a mangy
cat or a dog that's lost, or a fellow-creature down on
his luck, I always try to put meself in his place.
It's a weakness I've got.

Mr March. [*Warmly*] A deuced good one.
Shake——

D

He checks himself, but MR BLY *has wiped his hand and extended it.*

While the shake is in progress MARY *returns, and, having seen it to a safe conclusion, speaks.*

MARY. Coming, Dad ?

MR MARCH. Excuse me, Mr Bly, I must away.

He goes towards the door, and BLY *dips his sponge.*

MARY. [*In a low voice*] Well ?

MR MARCH. Mr Bly is like all the greater men I know—he can't listen.

MARY. But you were shaking——

MR MARCH. Yes; it's a weakness we have—every three minutes.

MARY. [*Bubbling*] Dad—Silly !

MR MARCH. Very !

As they go out MR BLY *pauses in his labours to catch, as it were, a philosophical reflection. He resumes the wiping of a pane, while quietly, behind him,* FAITH *comes in with a tray. She is dressed now in lilac-coloured linen, without a cap, and looks prettier than ever. She puts the tray down on the sideboard with a clap that attracts her father's attention, and stands contemplating the debris on the table.*

BLY. Winders ! There they are ! Clean, dirty ! All sorts—All round yer ! Winders !

FAITH. [*With disgust*] Food !

BLY. Ah! Food and winders! That's life!

FAITH. Eight times a day—four times for them and four times for us. I hate food!

She puts a chocolate into her mouth.

BLY. 'Ave some philosophy. I might just as well hate me winders.

FAITH. Well!

She begins to clear.

BLY. [*Regarding her*] Look 'ere, my girl! Don't you forget that there ain't many winders in London out o' which they look as philosophical as these here. Beggars can't be choosers.

FAITH. [*Sullenly*] Oh! Don't go on at me!

BLY. They spoiled your disposition in that place, I'm afraid.

FAITH. Try it, and see what they do with yours.

BLY. Well, I may come to it yet.

FAITH. You'll get no windows to look out of there; a little bit of a thing with bars to it, and lucky if it's not thick glass. [*Standing still and gazing past* MR BLY] No sun, no trees, no faces—people don't pass in the sky, not even angels.

BLY. Ah! But you shouldn't brood over it. I knew a man in Valpiraso that 'ad spent 'arf 'is life in prison—a *jolly* feller; I forget what 'e'd done, somethin' bloody. I want to see you like him. Aren't you happy here?

FAITH. It's right enough, so long as I get out.

BLY. This Mr March—he's like all these novel-writers—thinks 'e knows 'uman nature, but of course 'e don't. Still, I can talk to 'im—got an open mind, and hates the Gover'ment. That's the two great things. Mrs March, so far as I see, 'as got her head screwed on much tighter.

FAITH. She has.

BLY. What's the young man like? He's a long feller.

FAITH. Johnny? [*With a shrug and a little smile*] Johnny.

BLY. Well, that gives a very good idea of him. They say 'e's a poet; does 'e leave 'em about?

FAITH. I've seen one or two.

BLY. What's their tone?

FAITH. All about the condition of the world; and the moon.

BLY. Ah! Depressin'. And the young lady?

      FAITH *shrugs her shoulders.*

Um—'ts what I thought. *She* 'asn't moved much with the times. She thinks she 'as, but she 'asn't. Well, they seem a pleasant family. Leave you to yourself. 'Ow's Cook?

FAITH. Not much company.

BLY. More body than mind? Still, you get out, don't you?

FAITH. [*With a slow smile*] Yes. [*She gives a sudden little twirl, and puts her hands up to her hair before the mirror*] My afternoon to-day. It's fine in the streets, after—being in *there.*

BLY. Well! Don't follow your instincts too much, that's all! I must get on to the drawin'-room now. There's a shower comin'. [*Philosophic-*

ally] It's 'ardly worth while to do these winders.
You clean 'em, and they're dirty again in no time.
It's like life. And people talk o' progress. What
a sooperstition! Of course there ain't progress;
it's a world-without-end affair. You've got to
make up your mind to it, and not be discouraged.
All this depression comes from 'avin' 'igh 'opes.
'Ave low 'opes, and you'll be all right.

> *He takes up his pail and cloths and moves
> out through the windows.*

> FAITH *puts another chocolate into her mouth,
> and taking up a flower, twirls round with
> it held to her nose, and looks at herself
> in the glass over the hearth. She is
> still looking at herself when she sees
> in the mirror a reflection of* JOHNNY,
> *who has come in. Her face grows just
> a little scared, as if she had caught the
> eye of a warder peering through the
> peep-hole of her cell door, then brazens,
> and slowly sweetens as she turns round
> to him.*

JOHNNY. Sorry! [*He has a pipe in his hand
and wears a Norfolk jacket*] Fond of flowers?

FAITH. Yes. [*She puts back the flower*] Ever so!

JOHNNY. Stick to it. Put it in your hair; it'll
look jolly. How do you like it here?

FAITH. It's quiet.

JOHNNY. Ha! I wonder if you've got the feeling
I have. We've both had hell, you know; I had
three years of it out there, and you've had three

years of it here. The feeling that you can't catch up; can't live fast enough to get even.

FAITH *nods.*

Nothing's big enough; nothing's worth while enough—is it?

FAITH. I don't know. I know I'd like to bite.

She draws her lips back.

JOHNNY. Ah! Tell me all about your beastly time; it'll do you good. You and I are different from anybody else in this house. We've lived— they've just vegetated. Come on; tell me!

FAITH, *who up to now has looked on him as a young male, stares at him for the first time without sex in her eyes.*

FAITH. I can't. We didn't talk in there, you know.

JOHNNY. Were you fond of the chap who—— ?

FAITH. No. Yes. I suppose I was—once.

JOHNNY. He must have been rather a swine.

FAITH. He's dead.

JOHNNY. Sorry! Oh, sorry!

FAITH. I've forgotten all that.

JOHNNY. Beastly things, babies; and absolutely unnecessary in the present state of the world.

FAITH. [*With a faint smile*] My baby wasn't beastly; but I—I got upset.

JOHNNY. Well, I should think so!

FAITH. My friend in the manicure came and told me about hers when I was lying in the hospital. She couldn't have it with her, so it got neglected and died.

JOHNNY. Um ! I believe that's quite common.

FAITH. And she told me about another girl--the Law took her baby from her. And after she was gone, I—got all worked up—— [*She hesitates, then goes swiftly on*] And I looked at mine ; it was asleep just here, quite close. I just put out my arm like that, over its face—*quite* soft—I didn't hurt it. I didn't really. [*She suddenly swallows, and her lips quiver*] I didn't feel anything under my arm. And —and a beast of a nurse came on me, and said : " You've smothered your baby, you wretched girl ! " I didn't want to kill it—I only wanted to save it from living. And when I looked at it, I went off screaming.

JOHNNY. I nearly screamed when I saved my first German from living. I never felt the same again. They say the human race has got to go on, but I say they've first got to prove that the human race wants to. Would you rather be alive or dead ?

FAITH. Alive.

JOHNNY. But would you have in prison ?

FAITH. I don't know. You can't tell anything in there. [*With sudden vehemence*] I wish I had my baby back, though. It was mine ; and I—I don't like thinking about it.

JOHNNY. I know. I hate to think about any-thing I've killed, really. At least, I should—but it's better not to think.

FAITH. I could have killed that judge.

JOHNNY. Did he come the heavy father ? That's what I can't stand. When they jaw a chap and hang him afterwards. Or was he one of the joking ones ?

FAITH. I've sat in my cell and cried all night—night after night, I have. [*With a little laugh*] I cried all the softness out of me.

JOHNNY. You never believed they were going to hang you, did you ?

FAITH. I didn't care if they did—not then.

JOHNNY. [*With a reflective grunt*] You had a much worse time than I. You were lonely——

FAITH. Have you been in a prison, ever ?

JOHNNY. No, thank God !

FAITH. It's awfully clean.

JOHNNY. You bet.

FAITH. And it's stone cold. It turns your heart.

JOHNNY. Ah ! Did you ever see a stalactite ?

FAITH. What's that ?

JOHNNY. In caves. The water drops like tears, and each drop has some sort of salt, and leaves it behind till there's just a long salt petrified drip hanging from the roof.

FAITH. Ah ! [*Staring at him*] I used to stand behind my door. I'd stand there sometimes I don't know how long. I'd listen and listen—the noises are all hollow in a prison. You'd think you'd get used to being shut up, but I never did.

JOHNNY *utters a deep grunt.*

It's awful the feeling you get here—so tight and chokey. People who are free don't know what it's like to be shut up. If I'd had a proper window

even—— When you can see things living, it makes
you feel alive.

JOHNNY. [*Catching her arm*] We'll make you feel
alive again.

> FAITH *stares at him ; sex comes back to her*
> *eyes. She looks down.*

I bet you used to enjoy life, before.

FAITH. [*Clasping her hands*] Oh ! yes, I did.
And I love getting out now. I've got a fr——
[*She checks herself*] The streets are beautiful, aren't
they ? Do you know Orleens Street ?

JOHNNY. [*Doubtful*] No-o. . . . Where ?

FAITH. At the corner out of the Regent. That's
where we had our shop. I liked the hair-dressing.
We had fun. Perhaps I've seen you before. Did
you ever come in there ?

JOHNNY. No.

FAITH. I'd go back there ; only they wouldn't
take me—I'm too conspicuous now.

JOHNNY. I expect you're well out of that.

FAITH. [*With a sigh*] But I did like it. I felt
free. We had an hour off in the middle of the day ;
you could go where you liked ; and then, after
hours—I love the streets at night—all lighted.
Olga—that's one of the other girls—and I used to
walk about for hours. That's life ! Fancy ! I
never saw a street for more than two years. Didn't
you miss them in the war ?

JOHNNY. I missed grass and trees more — the
trees ! All burnt, and splintered. Gah !

FAITH. Yes, I like trees too ; anything beautiful,

you know. I think the parks are lovely—but they might let you pick the flowers. But the lights are best, really—they make you feel happy. And music—I love an organ. There was one used to come and play outside the prison—before I was tried. It sounded so far away and lovely. If I could 'ave met the man that played that organ, I'd have kissed him. D'you think he did it on purpose?

JOHNNY. He would have, if he'd been me.

> *He says it unconsciously, but* FAITH *is instantly conscious of the implication.*

FAITH. He'd rather have had pennies, though. It's all earning; working and earning. I wish I were like the flowers. [*She twirls the flower in her hand*] Flowers don't work, and they don't get put in prison.

JOHNNY. [*Putting his arm round her*] Never mind! Cheer up! You're only a kid. You'll have a good time yet.

> FAITH *leans against him, as it were indifferently, clearly expecting him to kiss her, but he doesn't.*

FAITH. When I was a little girl I had a cake covered with sugar. I ate the sugar all off and then I didn't want the cake—not much.

JOHNNY. [*Suddenly, removing his arm*] Gosh! If I could write a poem that would show everybody what was in the heart of everybody else——!

FAITH. It'd be too long for the papers, wouldn't it?

JOHNNY. It'd be too strong.

FAITH. Besides, you don't know.

Her eyelids go up.

JOHNNY. [*Staring at her*] I could tell what's in you now.

FAITH. What?

JOHNNY. You feel like a flower that's been picked.

FAITH'S *smile is enigmatic.*

FAITH. [*Suddenly*] Why do you go on about me so?

JOHNNY. Because you're weak—little and weak. [*Breaking out again*] Damn it! We went into the war to save the little and weak; at least we *said* so; and look at us now! The bottom's out of all that. [*Bitterly*] There isn't a faith or an illusion left. Look here! I want to help you.

FAITH. [*Surprisingly*] My baby was little and weak.

JOHNNY. You never meant—— You didn't do it for your own advantage.

FAITH. It didn't know it was alive. [*Suddenly*] D'you think I'm pretty?

JOHNNY. As pie.

FAITH. Then you'd better keep away, hadn't you?

JOHNNY. Why?

FAITH. You might want a bite.

JOHNNY. Oh! I can trust myself.

FAITH. [*Turning to the window, through which can be seen the darkening of a shower*] It's raining. Father says windows never stay clean.

They stand close together, unaware that COOK *has thrown up the service shutter, to see why the clearing takes so long. Her astounded head and shoulders pass into view just as* FAITH *suddenly puts up her face.* JOHNNY'S *lips hesitate, then move towards her forehead. But her face shifts, and they find themselves upon her lips. Once there, the emphasis cannot help but be considerable.* COOK'S *mouth falls open.*

COOK. Oh !

> *She closes the shutter, vanishing.*

FAITH. What was that ?

JOHNNY. Nothing. [*Breaking away*] Look here ! I didn't mean—I oughtn't to have—— Please forget it !

FAITH. [*With a little smile*] Didn't you like it ?

JOHNNY. Yes—that's just it. I didn't mean to—— It won't do.

FAITH. Why not ?

JOHNNY. No, no ! It's just the opposite of what—— No, no !

> *He goes to the door, wrenches it open and goes out.*

> FAITH, *still with that little half-mocking, half-contented smile, resumes the clearing of the table. She is interrupted by the entrance through the French windows of* MR MARCH *and* MARY, *struggling with one small wet umbrella.*

MARY. [*Feeling his sleeve*] Go and change, Dad.

MR MARCH. Women's shoes ! We could have made the Tube but for your shoes.

MARY. It was *your* cold feet, not mine, dear. [*Looking at* FAITH *and nudging him*] Now !

> *She goes towards the door, turns to look at* FAITH *still clearing the table, and goes out.*

MR MARCH. [*In front of the hearth*] Nasty spring weather, Faith.

FAITH. [*Still in the mood of the kiss*] Yes, sir.

MR MARCH. [*Sotto voce*] " In the spring a young man's fancy." I—I wanted to say something to you in a friendly way.

> FAITH *regards him as he struggles on.*

Because I feel very friendly towards you.

FAITH. Yes.

MR MARCH. So you won't take what I say in bad part ?

FAITH. No.

MR MARCH. After what you've been through, any man with a sense of chivalry——

> FAITH *gives a little shrug.*

Yes, I know—but we don't all support the Government.

FAITH. I don't know anything about the Government.

MR MARCH. [*Side-tracked on to his hobby*] Ah ! I forgot. You saw no newspapers. But you ought to pick up the threads now. What paper does Cook take ?

FAITH. " Cosy."

MR MARCH. " Cosy " ? I don't seem—— What are its politics ?

FAITH. It hasn't any—only funny bits, and fashions. It's full of corsets.

MR MARCH. What does Cook want with corsets?

FAITH. She likes to think she looks like that.

MR MARCH. By George! Cook an idealist! Let's see!—er—I was speaking of chivalry. My son, you know—er—my son has got it.

FAITH. Badly?

MR MARCH. [*Suddenly alive to the fact that she is playing with him*] I started by being sorry for *you*.

FAITH. Aren't you, any more?

MR MARCH. Look here, my child!

> FAITH *looks up at him.*

[*Protectingly*] We want to do our best for you. Now, don't spoil it by—— Well, you know!

FAITH. [*Suddenly*] Suppose you'd been stuffed away in a hole for years!

MR MARCH. [*Side-tracked again*] Just what your father said. The more I see of Mr Bly, the more wise I think him.

FAITH. About other people.

MR MARCH. What sort of bringing up did he give you?

> FAITH *smiles wryly and shrugs her shoulders.*

MR MARCH. H'm! Here comes the sun again!

FAITH. [*Taking up the flower which is lying on the table*] May I have this flower?

MR MARCH. Of course. You can always take what flowers you like—that is—if—er——

FAITH. If Mrs March isn't about?

MR MARCH. *I* meant, if it doesn't spoil the look

of the table. We must all be artists in our pro-
fessions, mustn't we ?

FAITH. My profession was cutting hair. I *would*
like to cut yours.

MR MARCH's *hands instinctively go up to it.*

MR MARCH. You mightn't think it, but I'm talking
to you seriously.

FAITH. I was, too.

MR MARCH. [*Out of his depth*] Well ! I got wet ;
I must go and change.

> FAITH *follows him with her eyes as he goes
> out, and resumes the clearing of the table.*
>
> *She has paused and is again smelling at the
> flower when she hears the door, and quickly
> resumes her work. It is* MRS MARCH,
> *who comes in and goes to the writing table,
> Left Back, without looking at* FAITH.
> *She sits there writing a cheque, while*
> FAITH *goes on clearing.*

MRS MARCH. [*Suddenly, in an unruffled voice*] I
have made your cheque out for four pounds. It's
rather more than the fortnight, and a month's
notice. There'll be a cab for you in an hour's time.
Can you be ready by then ?

FAITH. [*Astonished*] What for—ma'am ?

MRS MARCH. You don't suit.

FAITH. Why ?

MRS MARCH. Do you wish for the reason ?

FAITH. [*Breathless*] Yes.

MRS MARCH. Cook saw you just now.

FAITH. [*Blankly*] Oh ! I didn't mean her to.

Mrs March. Obviously.

Faith. I—I——

Mrs March. Now go and pack up your things.

Faith. He asked me to be a friend to him. He said he was lonely here.

Mrs March. Don't be ridiculous. Cook saw you kissing him with p—p——

Faith. [*Quickly*] *Not* with *pep:*

Mrs March. I was going to say " passion." Now, go quietly.

Faith. Where am I to go ?

Mrs March. You will have four pounds, and you can get another place.

Faith. How ?

Mrs March. That's hardly my affair.

Faith. [*Tossing her head*] All right !

Mrs March. I'll speak to your father, if he isn't gone.

Faith. Why do you send me away—just for a kiss ! What's a kiss ?

Mrs March. That will do.

Faith. [*Desperately*] He wanted to—to save me.

Mrs March. You know perfectly well people can only save themselves.

Faith. I don't care for your son ; I've got a young—— [*She checks herself*) I—I'll leave your son alone, if he leaves me.

Mrs March *rings the bell on the table.* [*Desolately*] Well ? [*She moves towards the door. Suddenly holding out the flower*] Mr March gave me that flower ; would you like it back ?

Mrs March. Don't be absurd! If you want more money till you get a place, let me know.

Faith. I won't trouble you.

She goes out.

Mrs March *goes to the window and drums her fingers on the pane.* Cook *enters.*

Mrs March. Cook, if Mr Bly's still here, I want to see him. Oh! And it's three now. Have a cab at four o'clock.

Cook. [*Almost tearful*] Oh, ma'am—anybody but Master Johnny, and I'd 'ave been a deaf an' dummy. Poor girl! She's not responsive, I daresay. Suppose I was to speak to Master Johnny?

Mrs March. No, no, Cook! Where's Mr Bly?

Cook. He's done his windows; he's just waiting for his money.

Mrs March. Then get him; and take that tray.

Cook. I remember the master kissin' me, when he was a boy. But then he never meant anything; so different from Master Johnny. Master Johnny takes things to 'eart.

Mrs March. Just so, Cook.

Cook. There's not an ounce of vice in 'im. It's all his goodness, dear little feller.

Mrs March. That's the danger, with a girl like that.

Cook. It's eatin' hearty all of a sudden that's made her poptious. But there, ma'am, try her again. Master Johnny'll be so cut up!

Mrs March. No playing with fire, Cook. We were foolish to let her come.

Cook. Oh! dear, he *will* be angry with me. If

E

you hadn't been in the kitchen and heard me, ma'am, I'd ha' let it pass.

MRS MARCH. That would have been very wrong of you.

COOK. Ah! But I'd do a lot of wrong things for Master Johnny. There's always some one you'll go wrong for!

MRS MARCH. Well, get Mr Bly; and take that tray, there's a good soul.

> COOK *goes out with the tray ; and while waiting,*
> MRS MARCH *finishes clearing the table. She*
> *has not quite finished when* MR BLY *enters.*

BLY. Your service, ma'am!

MRS MARCH. [*With embarrassment*] I'm very sorry, Mr Bly, but circumstances over which I have no control——

BLY. [*With deprecation*] Ah! we all has them. The winders *ought* to be done once a week now the Spring's on 'em.

MRS MARCH. No, no; it's your daughter——

BLY. [*Deeply*] Not been givin' way to 'er instincts, I do trust.

MRS MARCH. Yes. I've just had to say good-bye to her.

BLY. [*Very blank*] Nothing to do with property, I hope?

MRS MARCH. No, no! Giddiness with my son. It's impossible; she really must learn.

BLY. Oh! but 'oo's to learn 'er? Couldn't you learn your son instead?

MRS MARCH. No. My son is very high-minded.

BLY. [*Dubiously*] I see. How am I goin' to get over this ?   Shall I tell you what I think, ma'am ?

MRS MARCH. I'm afraid it'll be no good.

BLY. That's it. Character's born, not made. You can clean yer winders and clean 'em, but that don't change the colour of the glass. My father would have given her a good hidin', but I shan't. Why not ? Because my glass ain't as thick as his. I see through it ; I see my girl's temptations, I see what she is—likes a bit o' life, likes a flower, an' a dance. She's a natural morganatic.

MRS MARCH. A what ?

BLY. Nothin'll ever make her regular.   Mr March'll understand how I feel. Poor girl ! In the mud again. Well, we must keep smilin'. [*His face is as long as his arm*] The poor 'ave their troubles, there's no doubt. [*He turns to go*] There's nothin' can save her but money, so as she can do as she likes. Then she wouldn't want to do it.

MRS MARCH. I'm very sorry, but there it is.

BLY. And I thought she was goin' to be a success here. Fact is, you can't see anything till it 'appens. There's winders all round, but you can't see. Follow your instincts—it's the only way.

MRS MARCH. It hasn't helped your daughter.

BLY. I was speakin' philosophic ! Well, I'll go 'ome now, and prepare meself for the worst.

MRS MARCH. Has Cook given you your money ?

BLY. She 'as.

> *He goes out gloomily and is nearly overthrown in the doorway by the violent entry of* JOHNNY.

JOHNNY. What's this, Mother? I won't have it
—it's pre-war.

MRS MARCH. [*Indicating* MR BLY] Johnny!

> JOHNNY *waves* BLY *out of the room and closes
> the door.*

JOHNNY. I won't have her go. She's a pathetic
little creature.

MRS MARCH. [*Unruffled*] She's a minx.

JOHNNY. Mother!

MRS MARCH. Now, Johnny, be sensible. She's a
very pretty girl, and this is my house.

JOHNNY. Of course you think the worst. Trust
anyone who wasn't in the war for that!

MRS MARCH. I don't think either the better or the
worse. Kisses are kisses!

JOHNNY. Mother, you're like the papers—you
put in all the vice and leave out all the virtue, and
call that human nature. The kiss was an accident
that I bitterly regret.

MRS MARCH. Johnny, how can you?

JOHNNY. Dash it! You know what I mean. I
regret it with my—my conscience. It shan't occur
again.

MRS MARCH. Till next time.

JOHNNY. Mother, you make me despair. You're
so matter-of-fact, you never give one credit for a
pure ideal.

MRS MARCH. I know where ideals lead.

JOHNNY. Where?

MRS MARCH. Into the soup. And the purer they
are, the hotter the soup.

JOHNNY. And you married father !

MRS MARCH. I did.

JOHNNY. Well, that girl is not to be chucked out ;
I won't have her on my chest.

MRS MARCH. That's why she's going, Johnny.

JOHNNY. She is not. Look at me !

> MRS MARCH *looks at him from across the
> dining-table, for he has marched up to it,
> till they are staring at each other across
> the now cleared rosewood.*

MRS MARCH. How are you going to stop her ?

JOHNNY. Oh, I'll stop her right enough. If I
stuck it out in Hell, I can stick it out in Highgate.

MRS MARCH. Johnny, listen. I've watched this
girl ; and I don't watch what I want to see—like
your father—I watch what *is.* She's not a hard
case—yet ; but she will be.

JOHNNY. And why ? Because all you matter-of-
fact people make up your minds to it. What earthly
chance has she had ?

MRS MARCH. She's a baggage. There are such
things, you know, Johnny.

JOHNNY. She's a little creature who went down in
the scrum and has been kicked about ever since.

MRS MARCH. I'll give her money, if you'll keep
her at arm's length.

JOHNNY. I call that revolting. What she wants is
the human touch.

MRS MARCH. I've not a doubt of it.

> JOHNNY *rises in disgust.*

Johnny, what is the use of wrapping the thing up

in catchwords ? Human touch ! A young man like you never saved a girl like her. It's as fantastic as—as Tolstoi's "Resurrection."

JOHNNY. Tolstoi was the most truthful writer that ever lived.

MRS MARCH. Tolstoi was a Russian — always proving that what isn't, is.

JOHNNY. Russians are charitable, anyway, and see into other people's souls.

MRS MARCH. That's why they're hopeless.

JOHNNY. Well—for cynicism——

MRS MARCH. It's at least as important, Johnny, to see into ourselves as into other people. I've been trying to make your father understand that ever since we married. He'd be such a good writer if he did—he wouldn't write at all.

JOHNNY. Father has imagination.

MRS MARCH. And no business to meddle with practical affairs. You and he always ride in front of the hounds. Do you remember when the war broke out, how angry you were with me because I said we were fighting from a sense of self-preservation ? Well, weren't we ?

JOHNNY. That's what I'm doing now, anyway.

MRS MARCH. Saving this girl, to save yourself ?

JOHNNY. I must have something decent to do sometimes. There isn't an ideal left.

MRS MARCH. If you knew how tired I am of the word, Johnny !

JOHNNY. There are thousands who feel like me— that the bottom's out of everything. It sickens me that anything in the least generous should get sat on by all you people who haven't risked your lives.

MRS MARCH. [*With a smile*] I risked mine when you were born, Johnny. You were always very difficult.

JOHNNY. That girl's been telling me—I can see the whole thing.

MRS MARCH. The fact that she suffered doesn't alter her nature ; or the danger to you and us.

JOHNNY. There *is* no danger—I told her I didn't mean it.

MRS MARCH. And she smiled ? Didn't she ?

JOHNNY. I—I don't know.

MRS MARCH. If you were ordinary, Johnny, it would be the girl's look-out. But you're not, and I'm not going to have you in the trap she'll set for you.

JOHNNY. You think she's a designing minx. I tell you she's got no more design in her than a rabbit. She's just at the mercy of anything.

MRS MARCH. That's the trap. She'll play on your feelings, and you'll be caught.

JOHNNY. I'm not a baby.

MRS MARCH. You are—and she'll smother *you*.

JOHNNY. How beastly women are to each other !

MRS MARCH. We know ourselves, you see. The girl's father realises perfectly what she is.

JOHNNY. Mr Bly is a dodderer. And she's got no mother. I'll bet you've never realised the life girls who get outed lead. I've seen them—I saw them in France. It gives one the horrors.

MRS MARCH. I can imagine it. But no girl gets " outed," as you call it, unless she's predisposed that way.

JOHNNY. That's all you know of the pressure of life.

MRS MARCH. Excuse me, Johnny. I worked three years among factory girls, and I know how they manage to resist things when they've got stuff in them.

JOHNNY. Yes, I know what you mean by stuff— good hard self-preservative instinct. Why should the wretched girl who hasn't got that be turned down ? She wants protection all the more.

MRS MARCH. I've offered to help with money till she gets a place.

JOHNNY. And you know she won't take it. She's got that much stuff in her. This place is her only chance. I appeal to you, Mother—please tell her not to go.

MRS MARCH. I shall not, Johnny.

JOHNNY. [*Turning abruptly*] Then we know where we are.

MRS MARCH. I know where you'll be before a week's over.

JOHNNY. Where ?

MRS MARCH. In her arms.

JOHNNY. [*From the door, grimly*] If I am, I'll have the right to be !

MRS MARCH. Johnny !   [*But he is gone.

           MRS MARCH *follows to call him back, but is met by* MARY.

MARY. So you've tumbled, Mother ?

MRS MARCH. I should think I have! Johnny is making an idiot of himself about that girl.

MARY. He's got the best intentions.

MRS MARCH. It's all your father. What can one expect when your father carries on like a lunatic over his paper every morning?

MARY. Father must have opinions of his own.

MRS MARCH. He has only one: Whatever is, is wrong.

MARY. He can't help being intellectual, Mother.

MRS MARCH. If he would only learn that the value of a sentiment is the amount of sacrifice you are prepared to make for it!

MARY. Yes: I read that in "The Times" yesterday. Father's much safer than Johnny. Johnny isn't safe at all; he might make a sacrifice any day. What were they doing?

MRS MARCH. Cook caught them kissing.

MARY. How truly horrible!

          As she speaks MR MARCH *comes in.*

MR MARCH. I met Johnny using the most poetic language. What's happened?

MRS MARCH. He and that girl. Johnny's talking nonsense about wanting to save her. I've told her to pack up.

MR MARCH. Isn't that rather coercive, Joan?

MRS MARCH. Do you approve of Johnny getting entangled with this girl?

MR MARCH. No. I was only saying to Mary——

MRS MARCH. Oh! You were!

MR MARCH. But I can quite see why Johnny——

MRS MARCH. The Government, I suppose !

MR MARCH. Certainly.

MRS MARCH. Well, perhaps you'll get us out of the mess you've got us into.

MR MARCH. Where's the girl ?

MRS MARCH. In her room—packing.

MR MARCH. We must devise means——

> MRS MARCH *smiles.*

The first thing is to see into them—and find out exactly——

MRS MARCH. Heavens ! Are you going to have them X-rayed ? They haven't got chest trouble, Geof.

MR MARCH. They may have heart trouble.   It's no good being hasty, Joan.

MRS MARCH. Oh ! For a man that can't see an inch into human nature, give me a—psychological novelist !

MR MARCH. [*With dignity*] Mary, go and see where Johnny is.

MARY. Do you want him here ?

MR MARCH. Yes.

MARY. [*Dubiously*] Well—if I can.

> *She goes out.*
> *A silence, during which the* MARCHES *look at each other by those turns which characterise exasperated domesticity.*

MRS MARCH. If she doesn't go, Johnny must. Are you going to turn him out ?

MR MARCH. Of course not.   We must reason with him.

MRS MARCH. Reason with young people whose

lips were glued together half an hour ago! Why ever did you force me to take this girl?

Mr March. [*Ruefully*] One can't *always* resist a kindly impulse, Joan. What does Mr Bly say to it?

Mrs March. Mr Bly? "Follow your instincts"— and then complains of his daughter for following them.

Mr March. The man's a philosopher.

Mrs March. Before we know where we are, we shall be having Johnny married to that girl.

Mr March. Nonsense!

Mrs March. Oh, Geof! Whenever you're faced with reality, you say "Nonsense!" You know Johnny's got chivalry on the brain.

Mary comes in.

Mary. He's at the top of the servants' staircase, outside her room. He's sitting in an armchair, with its back to her door.

Mr March. Good Lord! Direct action!

Mary. He's got his pipe, a pound of chocolate, three volumes of "Monte Cristo," and his old concertina. He says it's better than the trenches.

Mr March. My hat! Johnny's made a joke. This is serious.

Mary. Nobody can get up, and she can't get down. He says he'll stay there till all's blue, and it's no use either of you coming unless mother caves in.

Mr March. I wonder if Cook could do anything with him?

Mary. She's tried. He told her to go to hell.

Mr March. I say! And what did Cook—— ?

Mary. She's gone.

MR MARCH. Tt! tt! This is very awkward.

> COOK *enters through the door which* MARY *has left open.*

MR MARCH. Ah, Cook! You're back, then? What's to be done?

MRS MARCH. [*With a laugh*] We must devise means!

COOK. Oh, ma'am, it does remind me so of the tantrums he used to get into, dear little feller!

> *Smiles with recollection.*

MRS MARCH. [*Sharply*] You're not to take him up anything to eat, Cook!

COOK. Oh! But Master Johnny does get so hungry. It'll drive him wild, ma'am. Just a snack now and then!

MRS MARCH. No, Cook. Mind—that's flat!

COOK. Aren't I to feed Faith, ma'am?

MR MARCH. Gad! It wants it!

MRS MARCH. Johnny must come down to earth.

COOK. Ah! I remember how he used to fall down when he was little—he *would* go about with his head in the air. But he always picked himself up like a little man.

MARY. Listen!

> *They all listen. The distant sounds of a concertina being played with fury drift in through the open door.*

COOK. Don't it sound 'eavenly!

> *The concertina utters a long wail.*

CURTAIN.

ACT III

ACT III

The MARCH'S *dining-room on the same evening at the
    end of a perfunctory dinner.* MRS MARCH *sits
    at the dining-table with her back to the windows,*
    MARY *opposite the hearth, and* MR MARCH *with
    his back to it.* JOHNNY *is not present. Silence
    and gloom.*

MR MARCH. We always seem to be eating.

MRS MARCH. *You've* eaten nothing.

MR MARCH. [*Pouring himself out a liqueur glass
of brandy but not drinking it*] It's humiliating to
think we can't exist without.   [*Relapses into gloom.*

MRS MARCH. Mary, pass him the walnuts.

MARY. I was thinking of taking them up to
Johnny.

MR MARCH. [*Looking at his watch*] He's been
there six hours ; even he can't live on faith.

MRS MARCH. If Johnny wants to make a martyr of
himself, I can't help it.

MARY. How many days are you going to let him
sit up there, Mother ?

MR MARCH. [*Glancing at* MRS MARCH] I never in
my life knew anything so ridiculous.

MRS MARCH. Give me a little glass of brandy, Geof.

Mr March. Good! That's the first step towards seeing reason.

> *He pours brandy into a liqueur glass from the decanter which stands between them. Mrs March puts the brandy to her lips and makes a little face, then swallows it down manfully. Mary gets up with the walnuts and goes. Silence. Gloom.*

Mrs March. Horrid stuff!

Mr March. Haven't you begun to see that your policy's hopeless, Joan? Come! Tell the girl she can stay. If we make Johnny *feel* victorious—we can deal with him. It's just personal pride—the curse of this world. Both you and Johnny are as stubborn as mules.

Mrs March. Human nature *is* stubborn, Geof. That's what you easy-going people never see.

> *Mr March gets up, vexed, and goes to the fireplace.*

Mr March. [*Turning*] Well! This goes further than you think. It involves Johnny's affection and respect for you.

> *Mrs March nervously refills the little brandy glass, and again empties it, with a grimacing shudder.*

Mr March. [*Noticing*] That's better! You'll begin to see things presently.   [Mary *re-enters.*

Mary. He's been digging himself in. He's put a screen across the head of the stairs, and got Cook's blankets. He's going to sleep there.

Mrs March. Did he take the walnuts?

MARY. No ; he passed them in to *her*. He says he's on hunger strike. But he's eaten all the chocolate and smoked himself sick. He's having the time of his life, mother.

MR MARCH. There you are !

MRS MARCH. Wait till this time to-morrow.

MARY. Cook's been up again. He wouldn't let her pass. She'll have to sleep in the spare room.

MR MARCH. I say !

MARY. And he's got the books out of her room.

MRS MARCH. D'you know what they are ? " The Scarlet Pimpernel," " The Wide Wide World," and the Bible.

MARY. Johnny likes romance.

> *She crosses to the fire.*

MR MARCH. [*In a low voice*] Are you going to leave him up there with the girl and that inflammatory literature, all night ?   Where's your common sense, Joan ?

> MRS MARCH *starts up, presses her hand over her brow, and sits down again. She is stumped.*

[*With consideration for her defeat*] Have another tot ! [*He pours it out*] Let Mary go up with a flag of truce, and ask them both to come down for a thorough discussion of the whole thing, on condition that they can go up again if we don't come to terms.

MRS MARCH. Very well ! I'm quite willing to meet him. I hate quarrelling with Johnny.

MR MARCH. Good ! I'll go myself. [*He goes out.*

MARY. Mother, this isn't a coal strike ; *don't*

F

discuss it for three hours and then at the end ask
Johnny and the girl to do precisely what you're
asking them to do now !

MRS MARCH. Why should I ?

MARY. Because it's so usual.   Do fix on half-way
at once.

MRS MARCH. There is no half-way.

MARY. Well, for goodness sake think of a plan
which will make you both *look* victorious.   That's
always done in the end.   Why not let her stay, and
make Johnny promise only to see her in the presence
of a third party ?

MRS MARCH. Because she'd see him every day
while he was looking for the third party.   She'd
help him look for it.

MARY. [*With a gurgle*] Mother, I'd no idea you
were so—French.

MRS MARCH. It seems to me you none of you have
any idea what I am.

MARY. Well, do remember that there'll be no
publicity to make either of you look small.   You
can have Peace with Honour, whatever you decide.
[*Listening*] There they are !   Now, Mother, don't
be logical !   It's so *feminine*.

> As the door opens, MRS MARCH nervously
> fortifies herself with the third little glass
> of brandy.   She remains seated.   MARY
> is on her right.

> MR MARCH leads into the room and stands
> next his daughter, then FAITH in hat and
> coat to the left of the table, and JOHNNY,

pale but determined, last. Assembled thus,
in a half fan, of which MRS MARCH *is the*
apex, so to speak, they are all extremely
embarrassed, and no wonder.

            Suddenly MARY *gives a little gurgle.*

JOHNNY. You'd think it funnier if you'd just come out of prison and were going to be chucked out of your job, on to the world again.

FAITH. I didn't want to come down here. If I'm to go I want to go at once. And if I'm not, it's my evening out, please.

            She moves towards the door. JOHNNY *takes*
            her by the shoulders.

JOHNNY. Stand still, and leave it to me. [FAITH *looks up at him, hypnotized by his determination*] Now, mother, I've come down at your request to discuss this; are you ready to keep her? Otherwise up we go again.

MR MARCH. That's not the way to go to work, Johnny. You mustn't ask people to eat their words raw—like that.

JOHNNY. Well, I've had no dinner, but I'm not going to eat *my* words, I tell you plainly.

MRS MARCH. Very well then; go up again.

MARY. [*Muttering*] Mother—logic.

MR MARCH. Great Scott! You two haven't the faintest idea of how to conduct a parley. We have —to—er—explore every path to find a way to peace.

MRS MARCH. [*To* FAITH] Have you thought of anything to do, if you leave here?

FAITH. Yes.

JOHNNY. What?

FAITH. I shan't say.

JOHNNY. Of course, she'll just chuck herself away.

FAITH. No, I won't. I'll go to a place I know of, where they don't want references.

JOHNNY. Exactly!

MRS MARCH. [*To* FAITH] I want to ask you a question. Since you came out, is this the first young man who's kissed you?

> FAITH *has hardly had time to start and manifest what may or may not be indignation when* MR MARCH *dashes his hands through his hair.*

MR MARCH. Joan, really!

JOHNNY. [*Grimly*] Don't condescend to answer!

MRS MARCH. I thought we'd met to get at the truth.

MARY. But do they ever?

FAITH. I *will* go out!

JOHNNY. No! [*And, as his back is against the door, she can't*] *I'll* see that you're not insulted any more.

MR MARCH. Johnny, I know you have the best intentions, but really the proper people to help the young are the old—like——

> FAITH *suddenly turns her eyes on him, and he goes on rather hurriedly*

—your mother. I'm sure that she and I will be ready to stand by Faith.

FAITH. I don't want charity.

Mr March. No, no ! But I hope——

Mrs March. To devise means.

Mr March. [*Roused*] Of course, if nobody will modify their attitude—Johnny, you ought to be ashamed of yourself, and [*To* Mrs March] so ought you, Joan.

Johnny. [*Suddenly*] I'll modify mine. [*To* Faith] Come here—close ! [*In a low voice to* Faith] Will you give me your word to stay here, if I make them keep you ?

Faith. Why ?

Johnny. To stay here quietly for the next two years ?

Faith. I don't know.

Johnny. I can make them, if you'll promise.

Faith. You're just in a temper.

Johnny. Promise !

> *During this colloquy the* Marches *have been so profoundly uneasy that* Mrs March *has poured out another glass of brandy.*

Mr March. Johnny, the terms of the Armistice didn't include this sort of thing. It was to be all open and above-board.

Johnny. Well, if you don't keep her, I shall clear out.

> *At this bombshell* Mrs March *rises.*

Mary. Don't joke, Johnny ! You'll do yourself an injury.

Johnny. And if I go, I go for good.

Mr March. Nonsense, Johnny ! Don't carry a good thing too far !

JOHNNY. I mean it.

MRS MARCH. What will you live on ?

JOHNNY. Not poetry.

MRS MARCH. What, then ?

JOHNNY. Emigrate or go into the Police.

MR MARCH. Good Lord ! [*Going up to his wife— in a low voice*] Let her stay till Johnny's in his right mind.

FAITH. I don't want to stay.

JOHNNY. You shall !

MARY. Johnny, don't be a lunatic !

> COOK *enters, flustered.*

COOK. Mr Bly, ma'am, come after his daughter.

MR MARCH. He can have her — he can have her !

COOK. Yes, sir. But, you see, he's—— Well, there ! He's cheerful.

MR MARCH. Let him come and take his daughter away.

> But MR BLY *has entered behind him. He has a fixed expression, and speaks with a too perfect accuracy.*

BLY. Did your two Cooks tell you I'm here ?

MR MARCH. If you want your daughter, you can take her.

JOHNNY. Mr Bly, get out !

BLY. [*Ignoring him*] I don't want any fuss with your two cooks. [*Catching sight of* MRS MARCH] I've prepared myself for this.

MRS MARCH. So we see.

BLY. I 'ad a bit o' trouble, but I kep' on till I see

'Aigel walkin' at me in the loo-lookin' glass. Then I
knew I'd got me balance.

> *They all regard* MR BLY *in a fascinated manner.*

FAITH. Father ! You've been drinking.

BLY. [*Smiling*] What do you think.

MR MARCH. We have a certain sympathy with
you, Mr Bly.

BLY. [*Gazing at his daughter*] I don't want that
one. I'll take the other.

MARY. Don't repeat yourself, Mr Bly.

BLY. [*With a flash of muddled insight*] Well !
There's two of everybody ; two of my daughter ;
an' two of the 'Ome Secretary ; and two—two of
Cook—an' I don't want either. [*He waves* COOK
aside, and grasps at a void alongside FAITH] Come
along !

MR MARCH. [*Going up to him*] Very well, Mr Bly !
See her home, carefully. Good-night !

BLY. Shake hands !

> *He extends his other hand ;* MR MARCH
> *grasps it and turns him round towards
> the door.*

MR MARCH. Now, take her away ! Cook, go and
open the front door for Mr Bly and his daughter.

BLY. Too many Cooks !

MR MARCH. Now then, Mr Bly, take her along !

BLY. [*Making no attempt to acquire the real* FAITH
—to an apparition which he leads with his right hand]
You're the one that died when my girl was 'ung.
Will you go first or shall—I ?

> *The apparition does not answer.*

MARY. Don't! It's horrible!

FAITH. I *did* die.

BLY. Prepare yourself. Then you'll see what you never saw before.

> *He goes out with his apparition, shepherded by* MR MARCH.

> MRS MARCH *drinks off her fourth glass of brandy. A peculiar whistle is heard through the open door, and* FAITH *starts forward.*

JOHNNY. Stand still!

FAITH. I—I must go.

MARY. Johnny—let her!

FAITH. There's a friend waiting for me.

JOHNNY. Let her wait! You're not fit to go out to-night.

MARY. Johnny! Really! You're not the girl's Friendly Society!

JOHNNY. You none of you care a pin's head what becomes of her. Can't you see she's on the edge?

> *The whistle is heard again, but fainter.*

FAITH. I'm not in prison now.

JOHNNY. [*Taking her by the arm*] All right! I'll come with you.

FAITH. [*Recoiling*] No.

> *Voices are heard in the hall.*

MARY. Who's that with father? Johnny, for goodness' sake don't make us all ridiculous.

> MR MARCH'S *voice is heard saying: " Your friend is in here." He enters, followed by a reluctant young man in a dark suit,*

> *with dark hair and a pale square face,*
> *enlivened by strange, very living, dark,*
> *bull's eyes.*

MR MARCH. [*To* FAITH, *who stands shrinking a little*] I came on this—er—friend of yours outside ; he's been waiting for you some time, he says.

MRS MARCH. [*To* FAITH] You can go now.

JOHNNY. [*Suddenly, to the* YOUNG MAN] Who are you ?

YOUNG M. Ask another ! [*To* FAITH] Are you ready ?

JOHNNY. [*Seeing red*] No, she's not ; and you'll just clear out.

MR MARCH. Johnny !

YOUNG M. What have *you* got to do with her ?

JOHNNY. Quit.

YOUNG M. I'll quit with her, and not before. She's my girl.

JOHNNY. *Are* you his girl ?

FAITH. Yes.

> MRS MARCH *sits down again, and reaching*
> *out her left hand, mechanically draws to*
> *her the glass of brandy which her husband*
> *had poured out for himself and left un-*
> *drunk.*

JOHNNY. Then why did you— [*He is going to say* : " *Kiss me," but checks himself*)—let me think you hadn't any friends ?   Who is this fellow ?

YOUNG M. A little more civility, please.

JOHNNY. You look a blackguard, and I believe you are.

MR MARCH. [*With perfunctory authority*] I really can't have this sort of thing in my house. Johnny, go upstairs ; and you two, please go away.

YOUNG M. [*To* JOHNNY] We know the sort of chap *you* are—takin' advantage of workin' girls.

JOHNNY. That's a foul lie. Come into the garden and I'll prove it on your carcase.

YOUNG M. All right !

FAITH. No ; he'll hurt you. He's been in the war.

JOHNNY. [*To the* YOUNG MAN] *You* haven't, I'll bet.

YOUNG M. I didn't come here to be slanged.

JOHNNY. This poor girl is going to have a fair deal, and *you're* not going to give it her. I can see that with half an eye.

YOUNG M. You'll see it with no eyes when I've done with you.

JOHNNY. Come on, then.

He goes up to the windows.

MR MARCH. For God's sake, Johnny, stop this vulgar brawl !

FAITH. [*Suddenly*] I'm not a " poor girl " and I won't be called one. I don't want any soft words. Why can't you let me be ? [*Pointing to* JOHNNY] He talks wild. [JOHNNY *clutches the edge of the writing-table*] Thinks he can " rescue " me. I don't want to be rescued. I— [*All the feeling of years rises to the surface now that the barrier has broken*]— I want to be let alone. I've paid for everything I've done — a pound for every shilling's worth.

And all because of one minute when I was half
crazy. [*Flashing round at* MARY] Wait till *you've*
had a baby you oughtn't to have had, and not a
penny in your pocket! It's money—money—all
money!

YOUNG M. Sst! That'll do!

FAITH. I'll have what I like now, not what you
think's good for me.

MR MARCH. God knows we don't want to——

FAITH. You mean very well, Mr March, but
you're no good.

MR MARCH. I knew it.

FAITH. You were very kind to me. But you don't
see; nobody *sees*.

YOUNG M. There! That's enough! You're
gettin' excited. You come away with me.

      FAITH'S *look at him is like the look of a dog*
        at her master.

JOHNNY. [*From the background*] I know you're a
blackguard—I've seen your sort.

FAITH. [*Firing up*] Don't call him names! I
won't have it. I'll go with whom I choose! [*Her
eyes suddenly fix themselves on the* YOUNG MAN'S
face] And I'm going with him!

                      COOK *enters.*

MR MARCH. What now, Cook?

COOK. A Mr Barnabas in the hall, sir. From
the police.

      Everybody starts. MRS MARCH *drinks off*
        her fifth little glass of brandy, then sits
        again.

MR MARCH. From the police ?

> *He goes out, followed by* COOK. *A moment's suspense.*

YOUNG M. Well, I can't wait any longer. I suppose we can go out the back way ?

> *He draws* FAITH *towards the windows. But* JOHNNY *stands there, barring the way.*

JOHNNY. No, you don't.

FAITH. [*Scared*] Oh ! Let me go—let him go !

JOHNNY. *You* may go. [*He takes her arm to pull her to the window*] He can't.

FAITH. [*Freeing herself*] No—no ! Not if he doesn't.

> JOHNNY *has an evident moment of hesitation, and before it is over* MR MARCH *comes in again, followed by a man in a neat suit of plain clothes.*

MR MARCH. I should like you to say that in front of her.

P. C. MAN. Your service, ma'am. Afraid I'm intruding here. Fact is, I've been waiting for a chance to speak to this young woman quietly. It's rather public here, sir ; but if you wish, of course, I'll mention it. [*He waits for some word from some one ; no one speaks, so he goes on almost apologetically*] Well, now, you're in a good place here, and you ought to keep it. You don't want fresh trouble, I'm sure.

FAITH. [*Scared*] What do you want with me ?

P. C. MAN. I don't want to frighten you ; but we've had word passed that you're associating with

the young man there. I observed him to-night
again, waiting outside here and whistling.

YOUNG M. What's the matter with whistling ?

P. C. MAN. [*Eyeing him*] I should keep quiet if
I was you. As *you* know, sir [*To* MR MARCH]
there's a law nowadays against soo-tenors.

MR MARCH. Soo—— ?

JOHNNY. I knew it.

P. C. MAN. [*Deprecating*] I don't want to use any
plain English—with ladies present——

YOUNG M. I don't know you. What are you
after ? Do you dare—— ?

P. C. MAN. We cut the darin', 'tisn't necessary.
We know all about you.

FAITH. It's a lie !

P. C. MAN. There, miss, don't let your feelings——

FAITH. [*To the* YOUNG MAN] It's a lie, isn't
it ?

YOUNG M. A blankety lie.

MR MARCH. [*To* BARNABAS] Have you actual
proof ?

YOUNG M. Proof ?   It's his job to get chaps into
a mess.

P. C. MAN. [*Sharply*] None of your lip, now !

> *At the new tone in his voice* FAITH *turns and
> visibly quails, like a dog that has been
> shown a whip.*

MR MARCH. Inexpressibly painful !

YOUNG M. Ah ! How would you like to be
insulted in front of your girl ?   If you're a gentleman
you'll tell him to leave the house. If he's got a

warrant, let him produce it ; if he hasn't, let him get out.

P. C. MAN. [*To* MR MARCH] You'll understand, sir, that my object in speakin' to you to-night was for the good of the girl. Strictly, I've gone a bit out of my way. If my job was to get men into trouble, as he says, I'd only to wait till he's got hold of her. These fellows, you know, are as cunning as lynxes and as impudent as the devil.

YOUNG M. Now, look here, if I get any more of this from you—I—I'll consult a lawyer.

JOHNNY. Fellows like you——

MR MARCH. Johnny !

P. C. MAN. Your son, sir ?

YOUNG M. Yes ; and wants to be where I am. But my girl knows better ; don't you ?

> *He gives* FAITH *a look which has a certain magnetism.*

P. C. MAN. If we could have the Court cleared of ladies, sir, we might speak a little plainer.

MR MARCH. Joan !

> *But* MRS MARCH *does not vary her smiling immobility ;* FAITH *draws a little nearer to the* YOUNG MAN. MARY *turns to the fire.*

P. C. MAN. [*With half a smile*] I keep on forgettin' that women are men nowadays. Well !

YOUNG M. When you've quite done joking, we'll go for our walk.

MR MARCH. [*To* BARNABAS] I think you'd better tell her anything you know.

P. C. MAN. [*Eyeing* FAITH *and the* YOUNG MAN] I'd rather not be more precise, sir, at this stage.

YOUNG M. I should think not! Police spite! [*To* FAITH] *You* know what the Law is, once they get a down on you.

P. C. MAN. [*To* MR MARCH] It's our business to keep an eye on all this sort of thing, sir, with girls who've just come out.

JOHNNY. [*Deeply*] You've only to look at his face!

YOUNG M. My face is as good as yours.

FAITH *lifts her eyes to his.*

P. C. MAN. [*Taking in that look*] Well, there it is! Sorry I wasted my time and yours, sir!

MR MARCH. [*Distracted*] My goodness! Now, Faith, consider! This is the turning-point. I've told you we'll stand by you.

FAITH. [*Flashing round*] Leave me alone! I stick to my friends. Leave me alone, and leave him alone! What is it to you?

P. C. MAN. [*With sudden resolution*] Now, look here! This man George Blunter was had up three years ago for livin' on the earnings of a woman called Johnson. He was dismissed with a caution. We got him again last year over a woman called Lee—that time he did——

YOUNG M. Stop it! That's enough of your lip. I won't put up with this—not for any woman in the world. Not I!

FAITH. [*With a sway towards him*] It's not——!

YOUNG M. I'm off! Bong Swore la Companee!

> *He turns on his heel and walks out unhindered.*

P. C. MAN. [*Deeply*] A bad hat, that; if ever there was one. We'll be having him again before long.

> *He looks at* FAITH. *They all look at* FAITH. *But her face is so strange, so tremulous, that they all turn their eyes away.*

FAITH. He—he said—he——!

> *On the verge of an emotional outbreak, she saves herself by an effort. A painful silence.*

P. C. MAN. Well, sir—that's all. Good evening!

> *He turns to the door, touching his forehead to* MR MARCH, *and goes.*
>
> *As the door closes,* FAITH *sinks into a chair, and burying her face in her hands, sobs silently.* MRS MARCH *sits motionless with a faint smile.* JOHNNY *stands at the window biting his nails.* MARY *crosses to* FAITH.

MARY. [*Softly*] Don't. You weren't really fond of him?

> FAITH *bends her head.*

MARY. But how could you? He——!

FAITH. I—I couldn't see inside him.

MARY. Yes; but he looked—couldn't you see he looked——?

FAITH. [*Suddenly flinging up her head*] If you'd been two years without a word, you'd believe anyone that said he liked you.

MARY. Perhaps I should.

FAITH. But I don't want him—he's a liar. I don't like liars.

MARY. I'm awfully sorry.

FAITH. [*Looking at her*] Yes—you keep off feeling —then you'll be happy! [*Rising*] Good-bye!

MARY. Where are you going?

FAITH. To my father.

MARY. With him in that state?

FAITH. *He* won't hurt me.

MARY. You'd better stay. Mother, she *can* stay, can't she?

                            MRS MARCH *nods*.

FAITH. No!

MARY. Why not? We're all sorry. Do! You'd better.

FAITH. Father'll come over for my things to-morrow.

MARY. What are you going to do?

FAITH. [*Proudly*] I'll get on.

JOHNNY. [*From the window*] Stop!

        All turn and look at him. He comes down.

Will you come to *me*?

        FAITH *stares at him.* MRS MARCH *continues to smile faintly.*

MARY. [*With a horrified gesture*] Johnny!

JOHNNY. Will you? I'll play cricket if you do.

MR MARCH. [*Under his breath*] Good God!

        He stares in suspense at FAITH, *whose face is a curious blend of fascination and live feeling.*

G

Johnny. Well ?

Faith. (*Softly*] Don't be silly ! I've got no call on you. You don't care for me, and I don't for you. No ! You go and put your head in ice. [*She turns to the door*] Good-bye, Mr March ! I'm sorry I've been so much trouble.

Mr March. Not at all, not at all !

Faith. Oh ! Yes, I have. There's nothing to be done with a girl like me.   *She goes out.*

Johnny. [*Taking up the decanter to pour himself out a glass of brandy*] Empty !

Cook. [*Who has entered with a tray*] Yes, my dearie, I'm sure you are.

Johnny. [*Staring at his father*] A vision, Dad ! Windows of Clubs—men sitting there ; and that girl going by with rouge on her cheeks——

Cook. Oh ! Master Johnny !

Johnny. A blue night—the moon over the Park. And she stops and looks at it.—— What has she wanted—the beautiful—something better than she's got—something that she'll never get !

Cook. Oh ! Master Johnny !

> *She goes up to* Johnny *and touches his forehead. He comes to himself and hurries to the door, but suddenly* Mrs March *utters a little feathery laugh. She stands up, swaying slightly. There is something unusual and charming in her appearance, as if formality had dropped from her.*

Mrs March. [*With a sort of delicate slow lack of*

perfect sobriety] I see—it—all. You—can't—help
—unless—you—love !

         JOHNNY *stops and looks round at her.*

MR MARCH. [*Moving a little towards her*] Joan !

MRS MARCH. She—wants—to—be—loved. It's
the way of the world.

MARY. [*Turning*] Mother !

MRS MARCH. You thought she wanted—to be
saved. Silly ! She—just—wants—to—be—loved.
Quite natural !

MR MARCH. Joan, what's happened to you ?

MRS MARCH. [*Smiling and nodding*] See—people
—as—they—are ! Then you won't be—disappointed.
Don't—have—ideals ! Have—vision—just simple—
vision !

MR MARCH. Your mother's not well.

MRS MARCH. [*Passing her hand over her forehead*]
It's hot in here !

MR MARCH. Mary !

         MARY *throws open the French windows.*

MRS MARCH. [*Delightfully*] The room's full of—
GAS. Open the windows ! Open ! And let's—
walk—out—into the air !

         *She turns and walks delicately out through
the opened windows ;* JOHNNY *and* MARY
*follow her. The moonlight and the air
flood in.*

COOK. [*Coming to the table and taking up the empty
decanter*] My Holy Ma !

MR MARCH. Is this the Millennium, Cook ?

COOK. Oh ! Master Geoffrey—there isn't a

millehennium. There's too much human nature.
We must look things in the face.

MR MARCH. Ah! Neither up—nor down—but
straight in the face! Quite a thought, Cook!
Quite a thought!

CURTAIN.